The BANK of Mom and Dad

MONEY, PARENTS, AND GROWN CHILDREN

DERRICK PENNER

Self-Counsel Press
(a division of)
International Self-Counsel Press Ltd.
USA   Canada

Self-Counsel Press acknowledges the financial support of the Government of Canada through the Canada Book Fund (CBF) for our publishing activities.

Printed in Canada.

First edition: 2014

Library and Archives Canada Cataloguing in Publication

Penner, Derrick, author
    The bank of mom and dad : money, parents and grown children / Derrick Penner.

(Personal finance series)
Issued in print and electronic formats.
ISBN   978-1-77040-213-3   (pbk.).—ISBN   978-1-77040-968-2 (epub).—ISBN 978-1-77040-969-9 (kindle)

    1. Parents—Finance, Personal.   2. Adult children—Finance, Personal. 3. Parent and adult child. I. Title. II. Series: Self-Counsel personal finance series

HG179.P45 2014   332.0240085   C2014-905622-2
                                             C2014-905623-0

Interview quotes by Richard Bell, Real Estate Lawyer, Bell
Alliance Lawyers & Notaries Public, used with permission.

Self-Counsel Press
(a division of)
International Self-Counsel Press Ltd.

Bellingham, WA	North Vancouver, BC
USA	Canada

Contents

Introduction   xi

Chapter 1
The Family Finances Discussion   1

   1. Be Open and Honest about Money Matters   4

   2. Tips for Discussing Money Matters   5

Chapter 2
Calculate Net Worth   11

   1. Retirement Road   16

   2. Create an Emergency Fund   16

Chapter 3
Give Your Kids a Financial Education   19

   1. Needs versus Wants   22

     1.2 The 24-hour rule   23

2. Track Daily Spending for Three Months 24

3. Prepare a Budget 25

4. Educate Young Adults about Credit Cards *i.e. don't* 29

5. Buying a Vehicle *use* 31

6. Cosigning Loans 34

7. Take Your Kids to a Financial Planner 35

Chapter 4
Taxes

37

1. American Gift-Tax Rules 39

2. Canadian Gift-Tax Rules 40

Chapter 5
Education

43

1. The Present Situation 46

2. The Future Situation 48

2.1 American 529 college savings accounts 49

2.2 Canadian Registered Education
Savings Plan (RESP) 50

3. Applying for Student Loans and Grants 52

3.1 The United States 53

3.2 Canada 54

4. Trade Schools and Other Options 56

Chapter 6
Property

59

1. Down Payment 64

1.1 American down payment considerations 65

1.2 Canadian down payment considerations 65

2. How to Make a Contribution to the Mortgage 66

3. Co-ownership 67

Chapter 7
Investments

71

  1. American Investments   74

  2. Canadian Investments   75

    2.1 Tax-Free Savings Account (TFSA)   76

    2.2 Registered Retirement Savings Plan (RRSP)   76

Chapter 8
Retirement & Aging — *boring*

79

Conclusion

85

Worksheets

1   Assessing the Adult Child's Financial Situation   6

2   Calculating Net Worth   14

3   Tracking Daily Spending   25

Notice to Readers

Laws are constantly changing. Every effort is made to keep this publication as current as possible. However, the author, the publisher, and the vendor of this book make no representations or warranties regarding the outcome or the use to which the information in this book is put and are not assuming any liability for any claims, losses, or damages arising out of the use of this book. The reader should not rely on the author or the publisher of this book for any professional advice. Please be sure that you have the most recent edition.

Note: The fees quoted in this book are correct at the date of publication. However, fees are subject to change without notice. For current fees, please check with the court registry or appropriate government office nearest you.

Prices, commissions, fees, and other costs mentioned in the text or shown in samples in this book probably do not reflect real costs where you live. Inflation and other factors, including geography, can cause the costs you might encounter to be much higher or even much lower than those we show. The dollar amounts shown are simply intended as representative examples.

Acknowledgments

Sometimes opportunities surprise you. I would like to thank Self-Counsel Press and Kirk LaPointe, Publisher and Editor-in-Chief, for bringing me into this project as well as Richard Bell of Bell Alliance Lawyers & Notaries Public and Lorne Goldman of Mac-Donald Realty, Lorne Goldman for their counsel and assistance.

Introduction

It's tough for young adults in North America these days — tougher than they thought, tougher than they were led to believe it would be growing up in the relatively affluent cocoon afforded to them by their parents during the 1990s and the 2000s (also known as the "oughts").

On the bright side, these young adults are educated — more of them have received college and university educations than ever before, traditionally the primary means of achieving social mobility. However, education is becoming increasingly expensive and they are earning those degrees and diplomas while racking up higher levels of debt than previous generations. As they graduate, they are entering a job market that is particularly unkind to the young. In both the United States and Canada, youth unemployment runs about double that for older workers. The young are presented with fewer full-time, well-paying jobs and more temporary contracts, part-time work, and frequent job changes.

Just as they are starting out with bigger debts and shakier career prospects, soaring property prices over the last 20 years have made it more difficult for the young to step onto the first rung of home ownership too. It's no wonder then that the young are remaining in the familial nest longer too. In the United States an estimated 36 percent of young adults between the ages of 18 and 31, the so-called millennials, live with their parents.[1] In Canada, it's a whopping 42 percent of those between the ages of 20 and 29 who either haven't left the nest, or have boomeranged back after completing a degree.[2]

Demographics and broader societal trends that have been developing over the last 50 years are likely driving many of the expectations now being placed on parents to keep extending financial assistance to their kids. At the heart of the parent and adult-child dynamic is the baby boom, the massive surge of population that emerged between 1946 and 1964 in a wave of optimism and incredible economic growth.[3] Across North America, there are 86 million so-called boomers — 76.4 million in the United States,[4] 9.6 million in Canada[5] — one-quarter of the continent's population.

The leading edge of the baby boom has begun hitting retirement age, but the bulk of the demographic is still well entrenched in the workforce and in their prime earning years. On aggregate, the wealth of baby boom has been a transformative force at all stages of their lives. That picture of wealth, however, might not be so apparent for a lot of individual families at the same time there is an increasing, broad-brush expectation that boomers will be able to come to the rescue of their kids.

On the other side of the generational divide includes the children of baby boomers — the echo, which comes out to be even larger. There are 91.4 million North Americans linked more or less with their boomer parents, those born between 1972 and 1992 — 82.2 million in the US, 9.1 million in Canada — a bit more than one quarter of the population.

1 "A Rising Share of Young Adults Live in Their Parents' Home," Pew Research: Social & Demographic Trends, accessed October 2014. http://www.pewsocialtrends.org/2013/08/01/a-rising-share-of-young-adults-live-in-their-parents-home/
2 "Family Life — Young Adults Living with Their Parent(s)," Employment and Social Development Canada, accessed October 2014. http://www4.hrsdc.gc.ca/.3ndic.1t.4r@-eng.jsp?iid=77#M_1
3 "The Baby Boom Cohort in the United States: 2012 to 2016," United States Census Bureau, accessed November 2014. http://www.census.gov/prod/2014pubs/p25-1141.pdf
4 "Age and Sex Composition in the United States: 2012," United States Census Bureau, accessed November 2014. http://www.census.gov/population/age/data/2012comp.html
5 "Generations in Canada: Age and sex, 2011 Census," Census in Brief, Statistics Canada, accessed November 2014. http://www.google.ca/url?sa=t&rct=j&q=&esrc=s&source=web&cd=2&ved=0CCMQFjAB&url=http%3A%2F%2Fwww12.statcan.gc.ca%2Fcensus-recensement%2F2011%2Fas-sa%2F98-311-x%2F98-311-x2011003_2-eng.pdf&ei=VKFiVLXQJMz20AT1s4KoDQ&usg=AFQjCNGKelFjwjReFL_cGOMZiM6tv7Hiow&bvm=bv.79400599,d.cGU

Call them Generation Y, or millennials, they can be forgiven if they have a jaded view of the world in front of them, considering that when they look back, they see parents, particularly baby boomers, who have managed to build up considerable wealth. It is the parents who have been the main beneficiaries of those skyrocketing property prices that have turned family homes into tidy nest eggs.

While Generation Y benefited growing up in households where family wealth and social mobility was rising, it is their parents who have hung onto the benefits while many of the younger generation struggle to find an independent foothold in society.

It can be difficult for parents too, after living through periods of unprecedented opportunity and economic growth, to think that their children might be the first generation that doesn't do better than they do. Before the kids even ask, parents might feel the pressure of guilt to offer a bit of financial assistance to help their kids take those first steps towards independence. Welcome to the Bank of Mom and Dad!

The transfer of wealth from one generation to the next has happened throughout history, but in recent years the transfer has taken different dimensions as one generation is finding it harder to get established. Instead of inheritance at the end of life, there is pressure to perhaps pass some of it along sooner, if that is possible. You may be asking yourself the following questions:

- Can you afford to give your kids some of their inheritance now?

- What is the best way to help them?

- Will the money you provide have stipulations?

- Will it be used to help build their careers with education?

- Is it to help your children acquire property at a time when they are struggling to save money?

- If your kids have managed to get through the journey from education, to career, to home ownership, but have sacrificed their own future investments along the way, should you help kick-start your children's retirement savings?

- Is your best strategy to focus on your grandchildren? If your children are having trouble building up education savings for their kids, a healthy contribution to a Registered Education Savings Plan (RESP) or college-savings plan might be the appropriate help from the Bank of Mom and Dad.

This is not to say that the older generations don't have challenges of their own. They may be wealthy on paper, but a high net worth doesn't translate directly into spare cash that they can spare for their kids. The modest family home bought a long time ago might be worth hundreds of thousands of dollars now, but that is not money that can be spent. Baby boomers in particular are also caught between the demands of two generations. Often referred to as the "sandwich generation," many boomers face the need to care for their own aging parents at the same time their kids are having a hard time getting out of the nest, which can stretch their finances at both ends.

Increasing numbers of North Americans don't have company pensions to fall back on in retirement. They might be under pressure to pay off mortgages and increase their own savings to make sure they can maintain a comfortable income in retirement, and worrying about getting their kids into a home should be the last thing they are thinking about. The cost of aging is another factor parents need to keep in mind as well. By the first decade of the 21st century, average life expectancy in the US had risen to 79 by 2010, compared with 74 in 1980; and 81 in Canada by 2009 compared with 75 three decades previously. It raises the specter of unexpected health-care costs that come with aging and longer periods of time in expensive assisted-living facilities.

The potential intermediary in all this is the expected transfer of wealth, some of which is happening now, from one generation to the next, and is forecast to continue over the next 20 years. Financial planners have attempted to stoke the excitement over this phenomenon the most, but estimates are that $8.4 trillion in inherited wealth will pass from one generation to the next in the US, and $1 trillion in Canada — seemingly enough money to repair any number of financial sins that have preceded its inheritors.

Inheritances, however, can be quickly spent before they are received and care must be taken not to build up assumptions and expectations about what inherited wealth can achieve.

Through the ages, children have always looked to their parents for help, advice, guidance, and even physical assistance in navigating life's challenges. Increasingly in the early decades of the 21st century, the expectation is that parents will help by becoming the Bank of Mom and Dad. This book is intended to guide parents in helping their children financially without going bust themselves.

Chapter 1

The Family Finances
Discussion

Many parents have already inadvertently become the Bank of Mom and Dad by default with children who are still living at home, or who have returned after attending college or university. Census data in both Canada and the United States show that more young adults are cohabiting with parents for longer. Providing children with a period of free rent and food can be a welcome relief to new graduates nursing significant student debts and uncertain job prospects. However, it is an arrangement that can strain the parents' day-to-day finances and is likely not a sustainable, long-term strategy.

The first step is to figure out if you can afford to continue offering financial assistance in a more formal way and for more definite goals. This is about establishing clear communications and not relying on assumptions about how well-off parents are or just how much money kids are making and spending. Adult children must decide what it is they need to get ahead, and parents need to be clear about exactly what they can and cannot do to help them.

The process can start with high and unrealistic expectations if you don't have a clear and specific understanding of each other's finances and what goals you are trying to meet. Both sides risk strained relationships if they leave room for assumptions that parents are simply wealthy enough to just pay for what the children need (and correspondingly, parents might overestimate just how much money adult kids are able to earn and save in temporary or part-time jobs). It is good to start with a definite and contained plan towards meeting clear and specific goals.

To the children, it might seem unfair that while they are struggling, they see parents who are comfortable and enjoying a better lifestyle than they are. Still lacking independence, they might feel entitled to the same kind of support they received from mom and dad while they were growing up. For the long-established parents living well within their means while also putting money away for future savings, the guilt at seeing their children struggle might make them want to offer support.

Parents shouldn't sacrifice their own financial health in the process, and children need to understand that. If parents are contributing to their children's immediate well-being, while the kids are appreciative, they may be spending money they should be saving. This is true especially the closer parents get to their own retirement and have less time to replace any savings they withdraw to help children, regardless of whether or not the kids pay back the assistance.

1. Be Open and Honest about Money Matters

Parents may know intuitively that they cannot afford to help if they are outright worried that they haven't saved enough money for retirement. They need to let their expectant kids know that and shouldn't be pressured into it. There needs to be a frank discussion about financial circumstances on both sides. Parents may appear to be well set to their kids, but they need to convey what their financial goals are and what they still need to contribute to investments and savings to get there.

Children need to do some reckoning of their own, being honest about their income and savings. This might involve creating more realistic budgets to determine what kind of resources they can contribute to whatever the goal is they decide to work towards. This may also wind up being a bit of an uncomfortable discussion about children living within their means. (See Chapter 3.)

Since this is about how to help adult children get a stronger foothold in life, it is preferable to talk about specific goals for doing so. Are you going to be contributing to the down payment for purchasing a first home? Or do the children really need assistance with the tuition for a particular educational credential that is going to advance their careers? Putting money into the purchase of a vehicle might qualify if the lack of their own transportation stands in the way of getting the jobs that they want, but might not if they just want a vehicle to get around and simply haven't put away enough money to do it themselves. Shelling out money that just winds up subsidizing the children's lifestyle isn't helpful.

Parents need to be clear about how the assistance is going to be offered. If they are able to extend financial help in the form of a gift, children need to understand that this is the case, and that it is going to be a one-time occurrence for the specific goal that you've both decided on. Parents may be tempted to offer help in the form of a loan, especially if they are worried about their own future savings. They might be more amenable to giving their children money if there is an expectation that this is just "bridge financing," and that the children will pay them back when they are on firmer financial ground. However, an educational credential might not get them into the desired jobs they want, and it might not lead to an increase in earnings they need to start paying back the loan. If a child loses employment, he or she might be at risk of not being able to pay back his or her parents for the down payment on that home they helped the child buy.

Even if both parents and the children understand that the assistance is a loan — even an interest-free loan — they should be prepared for the eventuality that the kids won't be able to pay them back. Parents should resist the temptation to use money that they cannot afford to do without later in their lives.

2. Tips for Discussing Money Matters

It is bound to be awkward, but if kids expect their parents to be forthcoming with financial assistance, the parents need to have an idea of where their children are financially. Simply laying out their student-loan totals to demonstrate how poor they are isn't enough information. You and the children need to figure out their overall financial situation. It cannot be a simple single question, "Here's how much I need for my goal, can you afford to pay it?"

If the kids were going to a bank for a loan, they would face a rigorous (some might argue privacy-testing) application process, and then wind up being denied. Just because they are turning to family for some financial help, doesn't mean they should be able to skirt past proving their need for help, versus their own income and resources. They should also be able to prove that the goals they are reaching for are pragmatic.

To get a realistic picture of what they are going to achieve, both parents and kids need to bring a certain amount of information to the table, and answer questions honestly. Documents such as the following will help illustrate an adult child's financial situation:

- Bank account statements.
- Investment statements.
- Credit card bills.
- Paycheck information.
- Tax return paperwork.

The adult children must not forget that they could be asking for a serious financial commitment that parents might want to establish in a formal, written agreement. This is not a polite conversation.

The kids should be able to answer the following questions in Worksheet 1.

WORKSHEET 1
ASSESSING THE ADULT CHILD'S FINANCIAL SITUATION

1. How much have you been able to save for yourself? For example, if you are asking for big-ticket help with the down payment for a home, you should be able to show what resources you are bringing to the transaction.

2. How much do you really earn? Your parents may understand that you are underemployed for whatever

qualifications you have, but you need to be honest about you income and how much help you really need.

3. What debts do you have? List every single debt you owe and the total amount as well as the interest. You parents might know about the student loan, and have an idea about your vehicle payments, but they need to know about credit cards and other consumer debts that are putting your financial situation at risk. You have to ask yourself whether it is really fair to seek your parents' help before you have paid off debts that are likely related to subsidizing your lifestyle.

4. What are your expenses (and are they realistic)? Your parents might look at you as a fashionably dressed adult, carrying the latest smartphone or gadgets, and wonder why they need to fork over money to look after some specific "need" while you seem to have no problem handling your "wants."

5. What is it that your parents will be paying for? If you're looking for help with tuition for education, you should be able to demonstrate how that credential or course will benefit your salary prospects.

6. Is this a loan you're asking for or a monetary gift?

7. If it is a loan, how do you plan on paying it back (e.g., monthly payments, yearly payments, whenever you can)?

As for question 7, parents should be looking for specifics such as amounts to be repaid, over what period of time, and if there will be interest added to the loan. It is important to commit this information to writing so there are no future misunderstandings.

For the adult child in this situation, he or she needs to know that the conversation is not simply a grilling from his or her parents to pry into his or her personal affairs. There are some very practical reasons to discuss the questions in Worksheet 1. For example, an adult child trying to buy a home might simply be focused on qualifying for a mortgage and hasn't thought about other expenses in the transaction, such as the closing costs and fees, renovations, and moving expenses. In talking about how much the adult child has saved, the parents might be able to give him or her tips on whether he or she has saved enough for the type of home the child is looking for or he or she is missing costs that will need to be paid for later.

Talking about the child's spending can be more about figuring what his or her attitude is towards money. It is also an opportunity for parents to gently (or perhaps more pointedly) point out where the adult child is spending money he or she doesn't need to and to have more resources than he or she thought to solve his or her own problems rather than looking for a handout from mom and dad.

Parents also need to be up front as well. If your kids are frustrated that you seem reluctant to offer them help, it could be because they really don't understand the family's financial situation. As the parents, you might be well-established in the family home that looks like it is worth a fortune (on paper at least), but the children might not be fully clued in to how much you are still paying on the mortgage, or whether you have already leveraged the home's value on a line of credit to look after needs of your own. Being able to show your kids your own financial picture — the money coming in, bills, and savings you are trying to set aside — demonstrates just how much room you do (or don't) have to offer help to your kids. They might not know and hadn't thought of it before, so it can be a lesson in both understanding and what they should be aiming to achieve themselves.

Young adult children should be able to understand that while their parents may not have batted an eye at shelling out $300 for a pair of athletic shoes their children demanded, they couldn't have justified that expense for themselves.

You may even discover that you've being shielding your children from the financial realities of the household. While it is natural to save your kids from the stress that goes along with managing personal finances during their youth, that doesn't help either party at this point. Parents have to come to grips with the knowledge that giving in to the pressure to keep giving their children handouts, it will only continue enabling — and entrenching — their kids dependence on them.

Also, armed with the knowledge of their parents' financial obligations, the kids might have a better understanding of the consequences that go along with what they are asking for. After knowing what it costs to run their parents' household, the kids might not bristle so much when they are asked to pay rent if they are still living at home in the house they grew up in, or be more willing to contribute to running that household in other ways such as through doing chores.

Chapter 2

Calculate Net Worth

Net worth is simply a calculation of what assets you've managed to accumulate, less the debts that you still owe. Calculating it, along with being clear about income, can contribute to a good baseline understanding of where everyone is starting. It's a very simple formula:

Assets - Liabilities = Net Worth

For adult children, there is a good chance that their net worth will work out to a negative number because of student debts and a limited number of years to accumulate savings. For parents, depending on how old they are, their net worth should give them a better indication of how close they are to meeting retirement goals and how much money they can provide to their children.

Financial institutions have tools that can help parents decide whether or not they can afford to give their children any money in the form of online net worth and retirement-saving calculators. For net worth, parents and children should each use Worksheet 2 in this chapter so everyone can see clearly where the others stand.

Online calculators ask users to punch in the details of their assets such as the following:

- Bank balances.
- Value of mutual-fund portfolios taken from investment statements.

- Estimated current value of the family home (often taken from property-tax statements).

Users are also asked to input the details of debts that they owe. The calculator performs the subtraction from assets automatically, and the number left over is the net worth on that particular day, assuming you could cash in and sell off your assets and pay off all of your debts. Most major banks, investment firms, and other financial institutions offer calculators among their online planning tools. Here are a couple of online calculators:

- RBC Royal Bank RRSP "Net Worth Worksheet" (http://www.rbcroyalbank.com/cgi-bin/retirement/networth/start.cgi)
- Bankrate "Net Worth Calculator" (http://www.bankrate.com/calculators/smart-spending/personal-net-worth-calculator.aspx)

The net-worth figure will change over time, but in the most recent statistics available, the median net worth of all Canadian families was found to be $243,800. However, in families where the highest income earner was between 55 and 64, the median net worth was $533,600. In the United States, the median figures were $139,000 for the households where couples were married and $240,000 for households where the parents were ages 55 to 64. See Worksheet 2.

WORKSHEET 2
CALCULATING NET WORTH

Assets	Amount
Nonregistered Assets	
Bank account balances	
Savings account balances	
Stock portfolio	
Life insurance cash value	
Tax refund	

Vacation pay (due to you)	
Other:	
Total Nonregistered Accounts	
Tax-deferred Accounts	
Retirement savings	
Education savings	
Pension savings	
Other:	
Total Tax-deferred Accounts	
Assets	
Vehicle:	
Vehicle:	
Home	
Cottage or recreational home	
Other (e.g., furniture, electronics):	
Other:	
Total Assets	
Total of Nonregistered Assets, Nonregistered Accounts, and Assets	
Liabilities	**Amount**
Vehicle loan	
Credit cards	
Rent/Mortgage	
Personal line of credit	
Student loans	
Taxes owed	
Other:	
Other:	
Total Liabilities	
Total Net Worth (Assets – Liabilities = Net Worth)	

1. Retirement Road

More importantly is for parties to figure out where they are headed, financially speaking. If one or the other does not have a good relationship with a financial planner, a retirement-savings calculator can be a helpful tool to get a snapshot of how well the parents might be able to withstand a financial gift or loan. For the kids, it could be a helpful illustration of how even modest savings can compound, especially when they start young.

Parents may well know where they are in their retirement planning, but this can be a good opportunity to explain it to their adult children. Pull out the pension, registered retirement savings plan, or 401K statements as part of that frank discussion about where parents and kids are with their finances to show their progeny how much retirement savings they've accumulated, and how much more they need to contribute before reaching their expected retirement date. It is also a way to get the kids thinking about that distant goal of their own retirement.

There is no easy answer to the question of how much people should be saving for retirement because it depends on each person's means and their expectations for retirement. Whether or not they are contributing to a company retirement plan will also influence how much more people should be saving. A long-standing rule of thumb says people should be trying to set aside 10 to 15 percent of their income for retirement, which is a good starting point for the sake of discussion. The end point also depends on what kind of lifestyle they want to maintain in retirement, and how long they expect retirement savings to last. Financial advisors suggest that a person will need 60 to 80 percent of their preretirement income to maintain their current lifestyle.

2. Create an Emergency Fund

Calculating net worth and evaluating their path toward retirement can be encouraging for parents who are well prepared, but seeing how far apart they are might be discouraging to their kids. While it is important to start thinking about building net worth and saving for retirement, kids need to focus more on immediate needs than fixate on that end goal before they've had a chance to get started. A good place to start is the concept of having an emergency fund. Discussion about proper financial planning will come later, but for the moment, raising questions about what kids would do in the case of a minor disaster. Consider the following questions:

- How would they handle an unexpected vehicle repair?

- How long would they be able to live on their savings in the case of a sudden loss of employment?

- What happens if a health emergency comes up and they can't work?

The answer to these questions comes down to the adult children's need for an emergency fund. An emergency fund gives both sides an immediate goal to focus on that can translate into resources for those long-term goals and a chance to build a lifelong discipline to be financially prepared.

It can be daunting in the beginning. How do you know what emergency is going to crop up? How much will it cost to fix or cope with the emergency? As a general rule, financial experts recommend aiming to set aside three to six months' worth of living expenses as a place to start as a helpful financial buffer to weather a financial rough patch.[1] Some suggest aiming for more such as eight months or longer. That can seem formidable in itself but there is an easy way to get there: Adopt the "pay-yourself-first" principle of saving.

The first step is to add up the following necessary monthly expenses:

- Rent or mortgage.

- Utilities including heat, power, phone, and cable bills.

- Debt servicing including student loans, vehicle payments, and any other outstanding credit (which is an opportunity to get adult children to confront more damaging forms of consumer debt such as carrying balances on credit cards).

- Insurance costs including health, vehicle, and rental/home.

---

1 "How to Weather the Financial Storms of Life: Preparing for Financial Problems," MyMoneyCoach.ca, accessed October 2014. http://www.mymoneycoach.ca/cgi/page. cgi/2/article.html/MyMoneyCoach_Blog/how-to-prepare-for-financial-problems-and-difficulties

- Groceries (this is a good chance to get kids thinking about the frugality of cooking basic foods at home versus dining out at restaurants).

The next step is to open a basic savings account (look for one that doesn't involve fees), which is separate from the checking account they spend money from that is attached to a debit card. Considering how much they earn, use that monthly expense figure to establish how much they can comfortably set aside per month towards meeting the emergency fund goal. Set up their checking account so that whenever they deposit a paycheck, an automatic transfer from their checking account will go into the emergency fund account. That way, they start saving without having to think about it, until they look at their bank statement to see how the money is adding up to meet that specific goal. After a while, they likely won't miss having the money in their checking account (and they will not have the temptation to spend it).

The practice of setting aside an emergency fund to handle living expenses for a given period while they are younger also gets young adults in the mindset of being prepared for other, bigger problems such as home repairs. A house or condominium isn't an everlasting thing. Roofs and siding weather and appliances break so home owners also need to set aside funds to replace the water heater that breaks down or replace shingles that will one day wear out. If they already have an emergency fund established, it is easier for young adults to expand it and plan for those bigger ticket expenses. Once they are able to adopt the "pay-yourself-first" principle of savings, it becomes the foundation for any goal the kids have in mind and a more independent attitude to perhaps hold off on future temptations to try and tap the bank of mom and dad.

Chapter 3

Give Your Kids a Financial Education

For many families, the tensions over finances and the impulse to borrow from the Bank of Mom and Dad may arise because the kids simply haven't learned enough about money. For parents, this is an unfortunate by-product of raising a worry-free generation in which children's needs were simply looked after. It isn't just about the paycheck that the kids earn and what they can spend it on. Understanding personal finances means learning how to budget, establish savings, and add to investments before spending. It involves learning about the responsible use of credit as a means to reach long-term goals, not to subsidize their lifestyle with pricey debt — especially high-interest credit cards. The end result is that adult children have to know how to live within their means.

The tension can be amplified if parents are caught between a child who has been financially responsible, is good at saving, and has not sought help; and one who hasn't caught on, is irresponsible with money, and seems to perpetually be looking for a handout. Such a dynamic between siblings can breed bitterness and lead to fights over wills and inheritances later when one or both parents die. This brings about another important reason for clear communications. Among kids, it is a good idea to make arrangements with the Bank of Mom and Dad a full family plan where everyone knows what is happening and each child is treated equitably. Giving the irresponsible child money without his or her sibling (or siblings) knowing about it can leave them feeling like it was done behind their backs and at their expense. Favoring one kid over another is never helpful.

At this stage, rather than money, the best gift parents can give their kids is a financial education. Money might seem like the solution to their problems, but kids have to know that just because their parents can help today doesn't mean they will be able to bail them out the next time they hit some trouble. Parents also need to avoid the temptation to try and ease their child's distress, which may be more imagined than real. They do the kids no favors by giving them handouts every time they ask if the kids haven't learned to stand on their own. For example, if both parents die tomorrow and they haven't taught their kids to be financially independent, how are these adult children going to cope with life?

1. Needs versus Wants

To live, people need a roof over their heads, food to eat, and clothes to protect them from the environment. To earn a living, they also need transportation to get to and from work. The catch is, they want their home to be luxurious with the latest furnishings and electronics, their food to include fine dishes from the latest trendy restaurants, and their clothes to be the most up-to-date styles and eternally new.

Young adults today have grown up in a consumer-driven economy surrounded by advertising and marketing aimed at stoking their desires for the latest smartphone, the newest flat-screen television, or video-game system. So much so that "I need that" becomes a common phrase when there is the release of the latest popular video game, fashionable shoes, or any other consumer item that is clearly and completely discretionary and not essential to the young person's existence. However, for young people used to having their expenses looked after, even into adulthood, the concept of delayed gratification and establishing priorities for their discretionary income is a distant concept. Even when discussing the difference between essential and discretionary, they may not understand the difference.

For adult children, starting on a conversation about wants versus needs might be uncomfortable and viewed by the kids as confrontational and poking into something that is none of their parents' business. However, if they are in the process of asking for a major financial commitment from mom and dad, they should be willing to confront realities about how they spend money. In a general sense, many young adults today do have a tougher time with unemployment and reduced expectations, but when they say their problem is that they don't earn enough, some of that could be because they're not in touch with how they are spending money.

Stopping to think about wants versus needs isn't a bad place to start. Even before approaching mom and dad to ask for financial help, if a young person is able to provide a clear picture of his or her financial responsibility to his or her parents, it will go a long way toward assuring them that he or she is asking for help toward independence, not continued dependence.

1.2 The 24-hour rule

If the adult children really want something, suggest they wait 24 hours before they purchase it. Also, help them create a list of needs vs. wants. It's amazing how many people get these two confused. You don't need that video game or those $300 sneakers (when you have five perfectly good pairs of sneakers getting dusty in the closet).

Ask them to try and abide by a 24-hour rule before deciding to buy something that they really want, but is completely discretionary. Did they really need those expensive new shoes because another pair is worn out beyond repair? Or are the shoes destined to sit in the closet only to be worn occasionally?

Foster the notion of delayed gratification. This means forgoing something frivolous now so they can enjoy something of greater value in the future. For example, going out to eat today would be enjoyable, but how would they feel about saving that money for a family trip later in the year? (The important point here is to actually set aside that money.)

Parents can remind kids of valuable lessons they learned from their own childhood. Most will likely have a recollection of a coveted toy they wanted as a child, and after playing with it once, the toy broke beyond repair. That truth carries over to adulthood for most discretionary things people purchase. Ornaments, knick-knacks, and trinkets are probably nearly worthless as soon as they leave the store. That stack of expensive video games isn't an investment that is going to earn a return — especially after next-year's new editions are released.

2. Track Daily Spending for Three Months

As people begin to think about needs versus wants, it is a good idea to start tracking daily spending — collecting receipts and writing expenses in a notebook, or better yet, on a computer spreadsheet. You don't know how much money you really have until you figure out where it is all going, and how spending on seemingly small things adds up. A $2.80 large coffee every morning, for example, might seem like a necessary pick-me-up before work and no big deal against a monthly paycheck. Extend that every day over a month, however, and it's about $85 per month or $1,022 over a year. Put in those terms and it is a more measurable portion of almost anyone's income and a figure relatable to other things. It can represent a winter coat that might be more of a need, or an airline ticket for the vacation that is a more highly valued want.

Track spending on everything — clothing, movie tickets, coffees, and nights out with friends at a pub or restaurant. Classify everything as wants versus needs. Even groceries can be broken down as such (which food items are ingredients for a meal versus junk food snacks). Nothing is sacrosanct.

Parents can help go through the ledger to zero in on items where the kid can easily reduce costs. For example, parents might know from experience that the child could replace that $85 per month coffee-shop habit with a $10 bag or two of ground coffee from the grocery store to make coffee at home. Or, if they're spending $6 per day five days a week for a sandwich at lunch ($120 per month) could be cut back to a dollar or two if they made a lunch at home to take to work. Worksheet 3 will help to see where money is being spent.

At the end of a month, separating wants and needs creates a visual picture of how much the young person needs to spend and how much of his or her money simply disappears into things he or she merely want and bleeds resources away from his or her real financial goals.

WORKSHEET 3
TRACKING DAILY SPENDING

Date	Item Purchased	Reason for Purchase	Want $ Amount	Need $ Amount
02/01/15	coffee	Craving	$2.00	
02/15/15	dress	Needed for work event		$75.00
02/18/15	movie and snacks	Wanted to see	$40.00	
		Total	$42.00	$75.00

3. Prepare a Budget

Tracking spending is the first step in establishing a proper budget, and a proper budget is simply a plan for someone to spend his or her income in a way that meets his or her immediate needs, long-term goals, and discretionary items that help make life enjoyable, but without going over the earned income.

You may have begun this process after the discussion of saving money for an emergency fund. A full budget will be an extension of that exercise in a more formal way. It will include the fixed expenses (e.g., rent, utilities, and insurance) and variable expenses (e.g., food, clothing, and discretionary items such as entertainment, alcohol, and personal grooming). A budget will include any debts that a budgeter needs to accommodate such as student loans, vehicle payments and credit card bills, and a portion that is set aside for personal savings. Savings start with the emergency fund, but will grow into the resources for other goals as a financial plan progresses. The goal is for all of that spending not to exceed the budgeter's income, aiming to even have a little bit left over at the end of each month.

On the surface it sounds like too many categories for one paycheck to handle, but there are some general principles that the young person should follow and financial advisors have basic guidelines to help young people establish what a reasonable budget should be for their given income. Credit Counselling Society of Canada maintains some excellent resources for budgeting and managing personal finances with the website MyMoneyCoach. ca. It includes guidelines to help people break down a spending plan for their net income (i.e., the amount left after deductions such as income tax).

Here is a suggested spending plan:[1]

- Housing — 35 percent: This includes mortgage (plus property taxes) or rent, insurance, electricity, and condo strata fees.

- Food — 10 to 20 percent: This includes groceries and personal care items.

- Clothing — 3 to 5 percent: This includes clothing for all family members.

- Transportation — 15 to 20 percent: This includes bus passes, taxi fares, fuel and insurance for a vehicle, insurance, parking, and an allowance for maintenance for things a budgeter knows are going to come up such as oil changes, new tires, and other servicing.

- Utilities — 5 percent: This includes heat or natural gas, phone and/or cell phone, cable, and Internet.

- Medical — 3 percent: This includes health-care premiums and other costs such as over-the-counter drugs.

- Debt payments — 5 to 15 percent: This includes student debt, vehicle payments, and consumer debts, which is an area that can squeeze the household budget when it exceeds recommended amounts.

- Savings — 5 to 10 percent: This is where young people start to set aside an emergency fund for unexpected expenses. However, as the emergency fund accumulates, they can devote portions of it to retirement savings plans or other financial goals.

---

1 "Budgeting Percentage Guidelines for Living Expenses: How Much to Budget for Cost of Living in Canada," MyMoneyCoach.ca, Credit Counselling Society, accessed October 2014. http://www.mymoneycoach.ca/cgi/page.cgi/2/article.html/Budgeting_Tips/How-Much-Money-You-Should-Spend-on-Living-Expenses-Budgeting-Guidelines-for-Income

- Personal and discretionary — 5 to 10 percent: Movie tickets, gym passes, tobacco and alcohol, dining out, other recreation, and hobbies.

Calculating the proportions might be an uncomfortable experience for the children. Their results might not seem to leave enough allowance for the movie they like to take in every week, or would cut into the amount they use for dining in restaurants. They should consider it another dose of reality to more sharply refine their sense of needs versus wants. No one says they shouldn't enjoy a decent lifestyle, but a decent budget is designed to show them the lifestyle that their income can afford, not afford them the lifestyle they think they deserve.

Keeping diligently to a budget should be some comfort to the parents that the child has the discipline to pay back any assistance that is offered as a loan, or that their contribution is going to be used for the stated goal that they've agreed to and won't simply be shoveled into the child's modern, consumer-oriented lifestyle.

Adult children living at home with parents rent free, even though they may be in their 20s, may still be shielded from the realities of what life costs. Again, this is where the willingness of parents to provide details of their own finances, such as the household budget, can help get their kids set up. Assuming the child is working, try to work out what are reasonable contributions to housing costs in the form of rent. Once the adult children have a clearer understanding of what the monthly grocery bills are, how much of that should they cover?

Mom and dad might not expect the adult children to pay specifically into the fund they are building up to put a new roof on the house, but they could certainly help with household maintenance such as mowing the lawn or landscaping. There should also be no question about putting gas in the family vehicle that they are borrowing.

For adult children who haven't spent any time living on their own yet, it might be a useful exercise to research and calculate a mock budget to get a better understanding of where they would fit into the society of their city. Look up apartment listings and even go look at a few to get a better understanding of how expensive it is to find a decent place to live that isn't in a bad part of town. Ask landlords about what utilities (e.g., heat, electricity, cable) they would be expected to pay and what the typical costs are for these services. Depending on where they live, they will be expected to pay a damage deposit, or even first and last month's rent up front.

Use these results to compute a budget document that includes the adult child's own variable costs such as clothing, food, and savings. It can add up to be another sobering look at real life compared with the paycheck that he or she is earning.

This is where a bit more parental experience can be a benefit. For kids who have generally been sheltered from the realities of what everyday necessities cost and how to get the best deals, mom or dad can step in with some coaching. Take the kids grocery shopping to show them how much it really costs to feed their family and how to effectively comparison-shop to get the best bang for their food-buying buck. Try also to coach grocery shopping in terms of meals served versus the cost of dining in a restaurant. You could take a restaurant bill, and then buy the ingredients to cook the same food at home (with leftovers to last through future lunches or dinners) to demonstrate how much money they can save.

For kids who are impulse-oriented purchasers, lead them towards sale flyers and coupons to show them how differences between regular prices and sale prices can be friendlier to the budgets that they are trying to establish. As parents guide their kids into leaving the familial nest, teach them that not everything has to be new when it comes to furniture, or even clothing. Yard sales and thrift stores, online classified listings or second-hand sellers can be great sources for them to find brand-name clothes and electronics at a fraction of the price of new, saving them money and bolstering their own financial resources for bigger financial goals.

Even if parents are generous enough to allow kids to remain at home rent free, these exercises should offer incentives to behave like adults and make adult contributions to running the household through upkeep of the house. Trade in the value of labor instead through housekeeping and yard maintenance.

Volunteering at a cause that is close to the family could be another contribution, especially if the young person isn't working. Kids, even adult children, can't respect reality if they've never lived it, so the purpose of such lessons is to come to grips with real life. If they're not coming to grips with reality, maybe the hard lesson is for parents to push their kids out of the nest. Ask them to leave if they aren't contributing because mom and dad need the space to look after their own financial goals.

4. Educate Young Adults about Credit Cards

Credit cards have a double edge to them. They've become ubiquitous, easy to get, and can offer young people an opportunity to earn a credit score. Using a credit card and paying the bill off every month on time is one of the best ways to build up a credit history that will stand them in good stead to apply for loans on major life purchases, such as a vehicle or even a home. Starting with a low-limit card (i.e., $500 or $1,000) that a child can be comfortable paying down regularly is a good way to start.[2]

The peril is that credit card debt can be among the most damaging forms of consumer debt. Not paying bills on time can damage the child's credit score and using the card to make big discretionary purchases that he or she doesn't plan on paying back right away can set up your adult child to pay punishing interest charges. There is the temptation to use a credit card to subsidize his or her lifestyle.

He or she might start with a lower limit, but it is not uncommon for the banks that issue cards to raise those limits as soon as the cardholder starts to build employment history. Having the limit raised to $2,000 might look like money that can be spent, but it in reality it is very expensive debt. Typically, banks charge annual interest rates in the range of 20 percent on balances that are not paid and carried over. One month worth of interest might not seem like a big deal, but those charges are added on to the card's balance each month it isn't paid and can compound quickly if the person winds up using the credit to make purchases that are over his or her budget. For example, a $500 balance from a discretionary purchase will add $8.33 to the bill the first month it is carried over, and after 6 months the $500 purchase has

2 "How to Establish & Get Credit in Canada: Credit Education," MyMoneyCoach.ca, Credit Counselling Society, accessed October 2014. http://www.mymoneycoach.ca/credit_rating/establishing_credit.html

racked up $52 in interest charges. After a year, the interest on the unpaid purchase would be $109. Max out a credit card at a $2,000 limit and the interest starts escalating at $33 per month to add $438 dollars to the balance within 12 months.[3]

Not paying off the bill regularly, carrying a balance, or even making late payments are all issues that will lower a person's credit score, which will hurt his or her chances of getting loans for any of his or her other financial goals. A credit score is an estimate of what the risk is that a borrower won't be able to pay back his or her loans. It is based on the borrower's past history with bill payments on credit cards, department store accounts, phone bills, and other forms of what are referred to as revolving credit. In Canada, credit scores will range from 300 to 900;[4] in the US, it is 300 to 850.[5] A score that is lower on either scale is bad because it indicates that the borrower is at a high risk of not being able to repay a loan. The higher the score the better it is indicating that the person is at a low risk to default on a debt.

Most banks, credit unions, and other financial institutions along with many retailers and specialty lenders offer credit cards with varying features. Consumers have hundreds of cards to choose from. Many cards offer rewards for using them such as points toward free travel, cash back, or free merchandise. The magazine *MoneySense* conducts an annual ranking of cards, which it advises that people choose a credit card carefully.[6] Rewards cards, especially travel reward cards, can be attractive and are a great option for consumers who have a disciplined habit of using the card in place of cash, but paying the balance off every month, making this a good option. However, many also come with annual membership fees and steep interest rates. A consumer who is worried about carrying a balance from time to time, or is only holding a card for an emergency, he or she is better searching for a card with a low-interest rate.

---

3 "Compound Interest Calculator," The Calculator Site, accessed October 2014.
   http://www.thecalculatorsite.com/finance/calculators/compoundinterestcalculator.php
4 "What Is a Personal Credit Rating in Canada: Credit Education," MyMoneyCoach.ca,
   Credit Counselling Society, accessed October 2014. http://www.mymoneycoach.ca/
   credit_rating.html
5 "Credit Bureaus and Credit Scoring," USA.gov, accessed October 2014.
   http://www.usa.gov/topics/money/credit/credit-reports/bureaus-scoring.shtml
6 "Canada's Best Credit Cards of 2014," Mark Brown, *MoneySense*, accessed October 2014.
   http://www.moneysense.ca/debt/credit-cards/canadas-best-credit-cards-of-2014

5. Buying a Vehicle

For young adults who haven't already taken on automobile ownership, buying a vehicle can be a considerable temptation as they reach the point of their own independence. For those still living with their parents and who have access to a family vehicle, the total cost of ownership might be another fact of life they haven't become acquainted with, even if they are diligent about keeping the gas tank full.

Manufacturers often advertise attractive offers on their popular vehicles that put a particular focus on a seemingly reasonable monthly payment, but one based on a fine-print list of assumptions that won't necessarily match the terms a new young buyer would be able to pay. While it might feel like a necessary accessory to get out on their own, buying a vehicle can be a challenging, or even a damaging, purchase at the same time they are trying to establish savings.

Vehicles are a conundrum in financial planning. Next to real estate, they're typically the most expensive things people will pour money into, but vehicles are no investment. A new vehicle is immediately worth less the moment you drive it off the lot and depreciation — that continuing loss of value — is the biggest cost that owners will absorb over the first five or more years of ownership.

Pouring gas into the tank is an apropos metaphor for almost all the ongoing costs that go into ownership. Insurance, tune ups, oil changes, parts and repairs, and even car washes will burn up a lot of the owner's money that he or she will never recover out of a depreciating asset. Yet automobiles do offer utility — transportation, which is a modern necessity. People do need to travel to get to work, to shop, or to take children to appointments. The question is, does the necessity of having that utility overcome the cost? Is the cost justifiable against the alternatives?

A good starting point is the budget that a young person should be establishing. The guideline is that transportation costs will account for about 15 to 20 percent of a person's income. To figure out if a vehicle fits into that equation, the person has to know the full cost of ownership (i.e., payments, insurance, fuel, and maintenance). If he or she is driving to and from work, add in parking and tolls where those are applicable.

Consumer advocates, such as the publisher of Consumer Reports, offer a considerable amount of help with estimates of the average annual cost to own a wide range of new vehicle models over the first five years of ownership, which can start at $5,000 per year for a small car and up to $11,000 for popular sport utility vehicles. Like adding up those small daily expenses over a year, calculating the cost of automobile ownership from the easily digestible monthly price quoted in advertising puts the magnitude of the expense into perspective against a young person's budget.[7]

In the United States, Kelley Blue Book, the well-known authority on vehicle pricing for consumers, similarly breaks down five-year ownership costs that show the financial impacts of ownership versus the purchase price, factoring in depreciation and financing, to show the quite considerable gap between the price of the vehicle and the money an owner can be expected to shell out, along with comparisons between the model someone wants and other, perhaps more cost-effective options.[8]

Because deprecation cuts so sharply into the value of an automobile in the first few years of ownership, a prospective buyer might want to consider buying a used vehicle. Let the original owner absorb the biggest hit in depreciation. Buying used brings in considerations other than a lower price. Important questions to sort out include how much mileage is on the vehicle (and does it have any warranty left), what is its condition, what is the last owner's repair history, and has it ever been in an accident? Searching the history of a vehicle's registration with provincial, territorial, or state licensing authorities is a worthwhile investment to double check the accident history, or confirm whether or not a previous lender has placed a lien on the vehicle for some reason. Paying for a mechanic's inspection can also be worth the expense to determine if there are any hidden repair surprises that haven't shown themselves to the previous owner. The last thing a prospective buyer needs, after believing he or she has saved money buying a used vehicle, is to spend thousands of

7 "What That Car Really Costs to Own," ConsumerReports.org, accessed November 2014.
   http://consumerreports.org/cro/2012/12/what-that-car-really-costs-to-own/index.htm
8 "What Is 5-Year Cost to Own?" Kelley Blue Book, accessed November 2014.
   http://www.kbb.com/new-cars/total-cost-of-ownership/?r=699495049417404500

dollars on an emergency repair that would have been spotted by an inspection. In researching used vehicles, sources such as Kelley Blue Book or Auto Trader offer good suggestions on what fair prices for used vehicles should be.[9]

However, for any vehicle, even used, the new buyer has to realize that unless he or she has saved all the money needed to buy it outright, the price tag is not the amount he or she will wind up paying for the privilege of being able to drive for transportation. As with any major purchase, it is advisable to run the figures (i.e., purchase price, interest rate, and term) through a loan calculator to figure out how much in additional interest will need to be paid. That is helpful to overcome the temptation of extending the length of time to pay off the principal as a means to reduce the monthly payment. That might seem to fit automobile ownership more comfortably into a tight budget, but that will have consequences in increasing the amount of interest he or she will pay, which is money that can be put to better use in savings.

For instance, borrowing $10,000 to buy a used vehicle with a loan that carries an interest rate of 5.5 percent, the borrower would pay $302 per month, and $871 in interest over a three-year term. Extend that to four years, the monthly payment is reduced to $233, but interest payments will add up to $1,163. Buyers might want to stop and think of what they'll do with an extra $292. Draw the loan out to five years, the monthly payment is reduced to a more budget-friendly $191, but the total interest increases to $1,461 — a full $590 more.[10] So, stopping to think, is it going to be worth it to take that amount of money out of the person's budget savings potential, knowing that he or she is buying something that will keep declining in value as long as he or she owns it?

Prospective borrowers also can't lose sight of the fact that a vehicle loan, like any other consumer borrowing, is considered negative debt as they reach for other life goals, particularly home ownership. For those who are also nursing considerable student debts, adding a vehicle loan to the equation can be damaging to the debt-servicing ratio that banks will look at in an application

---

9 "Guide to Buying a Used Car," AutoTRADER.ca, accessed November 2014.
  http://www.autotrader.ca/HowTos/BuyingAUsedCar.aspx
10 "Loan Calculator," Vancity, accessed November 2014.
  https://www.vancity.com/Loans/LoanCalculators/?xcid=pers_megamenu_loancalc

for a mortgage. Banks don't like to see more than a third of a household's income going into housing (which includes taxes and insurance) and more than 40 percent going to service all debt. Before borrowing money to buy a vehicle, they'll want to think of how much that debt will cut into that total ratio. It might make that more luxurious model, which appears to be more than a reasonable price, less of a reasonable deal than the more basic vehicle that will leave them more breathing room for housing options later.

After adding up the all-in costs of automobile ownership, the young person might be more willing to consider the alternatives of public transportation. Families living in bigger cities will have access to better public transportation — more frequent bus service and amenities such as rapid transit — that make it more palatable. While riding in a bus is less sexy than driving a fashionable automobile, the cost of public transit (i.e., $80 to $135 per month depending where you are in North America) can leave a lot more room in a budget to save money when a young person is just starting out.

Going over their finances together might be a tough, even an uncomfortable exercise for both parents and their kids, but it can be meaningful. To put the shoe on the other foot, parents might not be living by the best examples themselves, such as spending too freely on wants and subsidizing their own lifestyles with credit more than they want to admit. Both parents and kids could be approaching their respective financial futures with unhealthy assumptions about where their future income is going to come from, so the worst that can happen from a closer examination of their personal finances is that everyone gains a better understanding of their financial footing to move forward.

6. Cosigning Loans

A parent can help a child's application for a credit card, perhaps even a lower-interest card, by cosigning the application. However, cosigning carries risks for the cosigners[11]. Cosigning isn't a statement of equal responsibility. By signing an application, the child has to be aware that his or her mother or father has agreed

---

11 "The Dangers of Co-Signing: Credit Education," MyMoneyCoach.ca, Credit Counselling Society, accessed October 2014. http://www.mymoneycoach.ca/ credit_rating/cosigning.html

to assume the debt as his or her own if the child doesn't pay it back, which has consequences for the parent's credit score and credit report. It might not seem like a big deal on a low-limit credit card, but it starts to add up with late payments or if the child defaults. Cosigning becomes an even bigger concern if the parents are agreeing to back bigger-ticket loans such as for a vehicle or mortgage.

7. Take Your Kids to a Financial Planner

Establishing emergency funds and building regular savings into a budget are the first steps toward a long-term financial plan for the kids. Continuing the pay-yourself-first principle can be a powerful tool to move further down the path of savings and investment for their future financial independence, and perhaps lessen the burden on the Bank of Mom and Dad.

If parents have a good relationship with a trusted financial advisor, they will already have their financial circumstances laid out for them and a plan for reaching their own long-term goals, which will help them see how much room they have to offer their adult children assistance. At this point, it would be wise for parents to book an appointment to take their kids along for a meeting with their advisor to give them a realistic view of investments and how to plan for retirement and other goals. Asking an advisor for advice and using his or her experience to view the situation with unbiased eyes may help the adult children have a better financial understanding.

An advisor should be able to help clients plan their financial goals, such as setting a date for retirement and establishing how much they will have to contribute to investments in order to build up enough funds to meet them. Advisors who work for investment firms also must establish their clients' tolerance for risk and agree to an investing philosophy for managing their portfolio. In other words, establish whether the clients are comfortable with gambling some of their funds on higher risk purchases of stocks, or whether the clients are worried about losing money and more suited to conservative investments such as bonds[12].

---

12 "Financial Planning," GetSmarterAboutMoney.ca, accessed October 2014.
http://www.getsmarteraboutmoney.ca/en/managing-your-money/planning/financial-planning/Pages/default.aspx#.VE5auYfQf65

In this instance, parents will want to test their plan against the request of a child for financial help. Will devoting a significant portion of their savings compromise the goals that they've set? Even if the child pays them back, what would the parents be giving up in potential investment returns while the money is being paid back? How much longer would they have to work to replace investment funds if the child is unable to pay back his or her parents? Mom and dad might already have an idea of the answer, but it could be illustrative for the parents and child to go through the exercise with the advisor together.

Chapter 4

Taxes

The purpose of becoming the Bank of Mom and Dad is to give adult children a financial leg up, not deal either side an unexpected or complicated tax burden. Fortunately the tax implications are fairly straightforward, especially in cases where parents are able to offer assistance by way of gifts of straight after-tax cash.

There is one tax advantage for parents to pass on money as gifts sooner rather than later as an inheritance. Assuming that the gift is money outside of a parent's retirement-savings accounts, both sides can be better off giving it to their children now (if that was their intent) so that any returns earned on the funds are taxed at the child's lower income-tax rate and not the parents' higher rate. If children need the financial leg up, and aren't using a gift immediately, they will likely have more room to invest funds in tax-deferred accounts, or tax-sheltered accounts such as Roth IRAs in the United States and Canada's Tax Free Savings Accounts.

1. American Gift-Tax Rules

In the United States, there are annual limits on gifting money to individuals, but they will be more than generous for almost all families contemplating giving their kids a lift, and exceeding the annual limit likely won't trigger the federal gift tax; however, it will result in more paperwork at tax filing time.

For the most recent tax years, individuals can give up to $14,000 per year to each of their children — or anyone they want. For example, for a couple, that would mean $14,000 each for a total of $28,000 on which the child doesn't have to pay tax.[1]

The annual limit also applies if the gift is property the parents own that they want to transfer to their children. The transfer will be deemed to have been made at fair market value. However, exceeding the annual limit doesn't necessarily trigger a tax; it just means the donors must file a gift tax return along with their tax return (parents splitting a gift have to file anyway). The tax on gifts only comes into play if the donor's gifts add up to exceed the lifetime exemption, which as of 2014 was $5.34 million, which will not come into play for the vast majority of families seeking this advice.

For arrangements that are more complicated than a straight transfer of cash, it is a good idea to seek professional tax advice before proceeding with any agreement.

2. Canadian Gift-Tax Rules

As far as gifts of money to children go, Canada has the most straightforward rules: As long as parents are using their own after-tax funds to make a gift, doing so carries no tax implications for themselves, and under Canada Revenue Agency (CRA) rules — just like for lottery winnings or inheritances — children do not have to report gifts as income.

It gets trickier with loans, or if the gift is property that isn't a principal residence or some other asset that isn't cash. Even if no repayment is expected, from CRA's perspective, transfers will be deemed to have been made at fair market value — not the amount an asset was purchased for — which can trigger capital gains taxes. If parents are more inclined to offer financial assistance by way of a loan, it is still straightforward as long as they are using after-tax dollars and don't expect their children to pay interest on the money in repayment of funds. If they do expect their children to pay interest, that would be considered reportable income.

---

1 "The Estate Tax and Lifetime Gifting," Rande Spiegelman, accessed October 2014.
  http://www.schwab.com/public/schwab/nn/articles/The-Estate-Tax-and-Lifetime-Gifting

For arrangements that are more complicated than a straight transfer of cash, it is a good idea to seek professional tax advice before proceeding with any agreement.

Chapter 5

Education

E ducation is likely high on the list of options for discussion in asking for a withdrawal from the Bank of Mom and Dad, either the young adult looking for some help taking the next career step, or their older kids suggesting a bit of seed funding to start longer term education savings for their own children. There are strategies for addressing both ends of the equation, which will be discussed in this chapter.

Even for parents of kids who have already earned a degree or diploma, the topic of education shouldn't be discounted at the Bank of Mom and Dad because expectations are that today's young adults will change jobs, and even careers, more frequently than they have in the past, which will make the concept of lifelong learning more important. The job market in many parts of North America has changed so fast that young adults may have already reached the point of having to seek additional credentials after having already racked up considerable student debt.

Education is key to better careers and a more secure financial future for young people, but there are many ways to achieve the goals that young people want to attain. On the bright side, higher percentages than ever of North America's young people are taking on postsecondary education that it considered as a "rite of passage" for many families. On the downside, university and college have become more expensive leaving students with debts that make contemplating life's other big life goals a challenge — buying a home or starting a family. There are strategies for saving to minimize the debts needed to take on higher education, but it can involve a lot of research to plot a career path that both suits the young adults' interests and abilities and leaves them with education for jobs that are in demand.

Young people, who will likely be trading jobs and even careers more frequently than their parents did, will need to be more flexible in how they approach lifelong learning. Their career path might need to lean towards technical training, not university, and they need to remain open to the opportunities offered by the skilled-trades sector that is expected to need a big infusion of new talent in the coming decades.

1. The Present Situation

Young adults and their parents looking for advice on finding a firmer financial footing in the world have likely already had a first pass through the field of higher education with education savings plans, student loans that don't cover living costs, and summer jobs that don't yield enough savings to cover tuition. Higher education — college or university — has long been seen as a sure ticket to better jobs and upward social mobility in North America. For decades, this theory has been borne in studies showing that university and college graduates consistently outperform peers with only high school diplomas in terms of employment and earnings.

Today, however, young people are living through a certain dissonance with their experience. Believing they were on the right track, they've managed to accumulate crushing levels of student debt; for example, $1.2 trillion in student debts in the US, which is an average of $26,000 per graduate, with one in ten finishing undergraduate degrees with $40,000 in debt.[1]

In Canada, a now dated study estimated federal student debt totaled $15 billion and was accumulating at $1 million per day with an average student debt of $27,000.[2]

Young adults are graduating into a changing employment market where they aren't finding an easy fit between the skills

---

1 "How the $1.2 Trillion College Debt Crisis Is Crippling Students, Parents and the Economy," Chris Denhart, *Forbes*, accessed October 2014. http://www.forbes.com/sites/special features/2013/08/07/how-the-college-debt-is-crippling-students-parents-and-the-economy/
2 Student Debt in Canada: Education Shouldn't be a Debt Sentence: Canadian Federation of Students, accessed October 2014. http://cfs-fcee.ca/wp-content/uploads/sites/2/2013/11/Factsheet-2013-11-Student-Debt-EN.pdf

that they've developed and the jobs that are available.[3] Youth unemployment across North America has remained stubbornly high in recent years, running at close to double the rate of the rest of the population — 13 to 14 percent in late 2014.[4]

The next stop for many will be to search a more marketable credential or training to add to the young person's résumé. However, if the application to the Bank of Mom and Dad is about going for a master's degree, it might be an opportunity to open up more of a discussion about the child's career options. This is not a matter of simply saying no, but for mom and dad to encourage a child to more carefully consider what his or her goal is. Graduate school is a significant investment, but an advanced degree isn't always the credential that is going to pay off. To be a lawyer, the child needs to go to law school. To advance a career in business, a master of business administration can get a young person more quickly on the path to executive level. However, a master of art, or even a science degree, might not. Both kids and parents should be willing to put some work researching what the career and salary prospects for the desired credential versus the cost to attain the degree. Will it result in a job with better pay? How long will it take for the child to earn back what he or she and his or her parents have invested in an advanced degree?

For many, getting a university degree isn't all about getting on a specific career track. There are other, intangible, social benefits from higher education such as becoming more intellectually aware and concerned about global issues, for instance, or a better critical thinker. Of course, university graduates have typically, on aggregate, had lower levels of unemployment and higher levels of pay than their peers who simply graduated high school, but there is increasing evidence that the university premium is shrinking, particularly for those pursuing more general arts and social science degrees rather than credentials in specialized fields such as engineering or business.[5]

3 *Generation Jobless*, Dreamfilm Productions/CBC Doc Zone, accessed October 2014. http://www.cbc.ca/player/Shows/ID/2330990900/
4 Employment and Unemployment Among Youth Summary, Bureau of Labor Statistics, US Department of Labor (August 13, 2014), accessed October 2014. http://www.bls.gov/news.release/youth.nro.htm Labour Force Survey, August, 2014, Statistics Canada, accessed October 2014. http://www.statcan.gc.ca/daily-quotidien/140905/dq140905a-eng.htm
5 "Degrees of Success: The Payoff to Higher Education in Canada," Benjamin Tal and Emanuella Enenajor, CIBC Economics, accessed October 2014. http://www.google.ca/url?sa=t&rct=j&q=&esrc=s&source=web&cd=1&ved=0CBoQFjAA&url=http%3A%2F%2Fresearch.cibcwm.com%2Feconomic_ public%2Fdownload%2Fif_2013-0826.pdf&ei=wOVPVP6QFYSoyQTX24GoCw&usg=AFQjCNHgGkteMWGhJtyGbWKIZhiwZNm2BQ&bvm=bv.77880786,bs.1,d.aWw

The next step in education that is more likely to get a millennial into a better job will probably be in the form of specific occupation-related courses or technical training. The changing nature of the job market means that form of continuing education will be a recurring feature for today's young adults. A recent report from Human Resources Canada, the federal department responsible for employment programs, estimates average Canadians will work in three different career fields and eight jobs during their lives.[6]

In the US, the Bureau of Labor Statistics estimates that the typical American will stay in each of his or her jobs for just over four years, but for those born between 1979 and 1997, that figure drops to an average of three years.[7]

Expect charting a career path to be a longer journey with more than one destination, and some unexpected stops along the way. The jobs in demand are not necessarily what kids and their parents would have expected. A shrinking manufacturing sector in North America means less stable employment in factories, but an aging workforce means that occupations in the trades are increasing. Plumbers, electricians, carpenters, and other skilled occupations are expected to retire in the coming years, which will create new opportunities for younger workers, and not just in skilled work, but entrepreneurship as well. (See section **3.**)

2. The Future Situation

For many parents, shifting their focus to the generation beyond their children to the grandchildren will be something to think about. Their kids are finished with education, have stable employment, and have managed to take on home ownership, but where they could use some help is establishing savings plans that get their own children on a path towards a secure future. Tuition fees at colleges and universities have climbed in recent years leaving the parents of young children, familiar themselves with the challenges of student debt, wondering what postsecondary education is going to cost when their own progeny are ready to

6 "Continuing Education: A Conduit to a New Career," Rachel Aiello, *Career Options Magazine*, accessed October 2014. http://www.careeroptionsmagazine.com/articles/continuing-education-a-conduit-to-a-new-career/
7 "Job Hopping Is the 'New Normal' for Millennial: Three Ways to Prevent a Human Resource Nightmare," Jeanne Meister, *Forbes*, accessed October 2014. http://www.forbes.com/sites/jeannemeister/2012/08/14/job-hopping-is-the-new-normal-for-millennials-three-ways-to-prevent- a-human-resource-nightmare/

decide whether to take it on and just how they are going to pay for it.

This brings savings tools such as 529 college savings accounts in the United States (see section **2.1**), or Registered Education Savings Plans (RESPs) in Canada (see section **2.2**), which is where grandparents might prefer to deposit gifts of cash. There are substantial differences in how the plans work in each country, but the end result is intended to be the same: Upfront savings to cover significant portions of the cost of postsecondary education so the beneficiaries aren't taking on the massive debts that their parents did to earn a degree. In all instances, it is easy for grandparents to be involved in the process.

2.1 American 529 college savings accounts

This type of savings account takes its name from Section 529 of the US Internal Revenue Code; 529 college savings accounts are the central tool for postsecondary education savings in the United States. These 529 plans are typically sponsored by state governments or by educational institutions.

There are two kinds of 529 plans:

- Pre-paid tuition plans, which essentially allow the account holder to buy credits toward future tuition fees (and sometimes room and board) at guaranteed rates. The pre-paid plans are typically sponsored by state governments for the benefit of residents who plan to attend state colleges.

- College savings plans, which allows the account holder a wider range of options for investing contributions, such as in stocks or mutual funds, and can be used at any college or university. Withdrawals can be used for any eligible college expense, including living expenses.

Anyone can set up a 529 account for a beneficiary so it is something grandparents can do to give their adult kids a financial leg up with their financial goals. However, the withdrawals from the 529 are tax-free as long as they are used to pay eligible college expenses.

The list of eligible institutions where 529 distributions can be used extends to vocational schools and other postsecondary institutions so the beneficiaries don't have to face the pressure of having to commit to planning for college while they are growing up. However, withdrawals that are not used for eligible expenses will be subject to income tax, plus an additional 10 percent federal tax on the returns earned by funds within the 529 account.

Setting up a 529 account can be a relatively simple affair, but as with any financial commitment, it should be approached with careful planning. Grandparents might be able to set them up on their own, but if it is a measure designed to give their adult children a bit of financial relief, it is a good idea to bring education savings into a broader discussion about everyone's financial goals. While mom and dad might look at the account as a nice surprise for their kids to help with the future education of their grandchildren, the kids might have other more pressing needs where assistance would be more beneficial for the entire family. As with any assistance from the Bank of Mom and Dad, it should be offered through a process of clear communication.

2.2 Canadian Registered Education Savings Plan (RESP)

For a Canadian Registered Education Savings Plan (RESP), parents don't even need to be involved: Anyone can set up a registered account on behalf of one or more beneficiaries, and the federal government will even help by contributing cash through the Canada Education Savings Grants program.[8]

Those opening RESP accounts are known as "subscribers," and the institutions that offer them are called "promoters," which include most of the country's major banks, credit unions, and other financial institutions and investment funds.

If grandparents want to start an account, they subscribe through one of the promoters available and begin making contributions. Anyone can pay into the RESP. Contributions are not tax deductible, but the income generated by the RESP accumulate tax free while the beneficiaries are growing up. The beneficiary has to report withdrawals taken from an RESP, known as education-assistance payments, as income on his or her tax return, but any taxes will be at the young person's (presumably low) tax rate. If the beneficiary decides not to carry on to

---

8 "Registered Education Savings Plans (RESPs)," Canada Revenue Agency, accessed October 2014. http://www.cra-arc.gc.ca/tx/ndvdls/tpcs/resp-reee/menu-eng.html

a qualified educational institution, contributions go back to the subscribers tax free as well, since they came from their after-tax dollars in the first place.

If parents are setting up RESPs for their children, they are an easy place for grandparents to make one-time, lump-sum contributions since there are no annual limits on RESP contributions, but there is a lifetime limit of $50,000 for total contributions per beneficiary.

A RESP beneficiary doesn't have to immediately enter post-secondary education after finishing high school in order to tap into the funds, so parents or grandparents can continue to contribute as they enter their 20s if they haven't managed to hit the maximum by the time the young person is ready for university. However, RESPs do have a limited lifespan. Contributions can be made up to the 31st anniversary of the RESP being established, and beneficiaries must be withdrawing the funds as educational assistance payments (EAPs) by the 35th anniversary.

In an additional boost, the federal government contributes through the Canada Education Savings Grants program.[9] Depending on a family's income, the government will chip in a percentage of annual contributions made to an RESP to a lifetime maximum of $7,200 for each beneficiary.

One factor that is important for subscribers to keep in mind is that there may or may not be fees involved in managing the RESP funds, depending on how subscribers choose to invest the funds. Putting the money into stocks will mean paying commissions on stock trades as will buying mutual funds. Mutual funds will also charge for management expenses, so it is important to understand what fees will be involved in any funds that are chosen, and how that might eat into returns available to be paid out in EAPs. Promoters that are scholarship-plan dealers may also charge certain fees, such as commissions for salespeople or annual administration fees that subscribers might not be able to recover if the RESP winds up not being used and the contributions are returned.[10]

---

9 "Canada Education Savings Grants (CESG)," Canada Revenue Agency, accessed October 2014. http://www.cra-arc.gc.ca/tx/ndvdls/tpcs/resp-reee/cesp-pcee/csg-eng.html
10 "RESP Fees," GetSmarterAboutMoney.ca, accessed October 2014. http://www.getsmarter aboutmoney.ca/en/managing-your-money/investing/resps-for-education/Pages/RESP-fees.aspx#.VEFpZsnp98F

3. Applying for Student Loans and Grants

Student loans, grants, or bursaries are all sources of funds that may or may not be accessible to the continuing student. However, it isn't all about finding the cash to defray the cost of a further education. The process of applying for loans or bursaries can help the kid's sense of his or her own investment in what he or she is doing next. Completing the forms and assembling the documentation required in applications for financial aid such as transcripts, references, and other letters can test the young person's resolve. If those applications are successful and yield funds, that can instill more of a sense of responsibility to make the investment in time and effort pay off with good grades.

Regardless of whether a student is heading to a financial institution for the first time right after high school or is returning for additional credits and credentials, colleges and universities will have lists of scholarships and bursaries that students can apply for. Some will be program specific and based on merit while others will be based on financial need. Both federal governments and state or provincial governments also offer student assistance other than loans.

Student debt has become a bigger public issue for the increasing magnitude of the obligations that young people are taking on that can set them back at the start of their work life. Generally speaking though, as a concept, student loans aren't viewed as negative debt. Like a mortgage can be used to secure an asset that offers the borrower wealth-building equity over time, a student loan can be viewed as an investment that yields a return in higher income and better job prospects over the borrower's career. The payoff can come more quickly for students entering high-demand fields. However, before students overextend themselves, it is always advisable to search all the options available to them to defray the costs of education.

For parents of adult children who haven't yet delved into their postsecondary possibilities, starting out by helping kids research all the sources of financial assistance available to them can be a reassuring exercise. It lets them know that they aren't facing all of the costs of higher education alone. Reviewing the lists of scholarships and bursaries available for specific programs can enlighten both parents and children about those areas of study that offer better career prospects. Where there is high demand, there will be additional resources devoted to cultivating the best new recruits. As well, certain state and provincial or territorial aid programs show that governments are willing to invest in sectors where there is a brighter future in employment.

3.1 The United States

In the United States, the starting point for federal and state programs is the Free Application for Federal Student Aid (FAFSA),[11] which is used to determine a student's eligibility for federal student grants, loans, or work-study jobs. Programs are detailed online by the Federal Student Aid office, which is part of the US Department of Education. The application process calculates the student's cost to attend an institution and subtracts any expected family contribution toward cost to establish need.

Aid includes the Federal Pell Grant Program[12] for college undergraduate students in need, which will pay students up to $5,730 per year (as of the 2014 to 2015 school year). The Federal Supplemental Educational Opportunity Grant (FSEOG)[13] is paid to students with extraordinary need; however, it is administered by individual institutions, which receive funds from the US Department of Education's office of Federal Student Aid department, and pays students from $100 to $4,000 per year based on needs, their other awards, and availability of funds at a particular institution.

Also determined by the FAFSA application is the eligibility for Teacher Education Assistance for College and Higher Education (TEACH) Grants[14] and the Iraq and Afghanistan Service Grants[15] for students who have suffered the death of a parent due to military service in Iraq or Afghanistan.

11 "Apply for Aid," Federal Student Aid, US Department of Education, accessed November 2014. https://studentaid.ed.gov/fafsa
12 "Federal Pell Grant," Federal Student Aid, US Department of Education, accessed November 2014. https://studentaid.ed.gov/types/grants-scholarships/pell
13 "Federal Supplemental Educational Opportunity Grant," Federal Student Aid, US Department of Education, accessed November 2014. https://studentaid.ed.gov/types/grants-scholarships/fseog
14 "Teacher Education Assistance for College and Higher Education Grant," Federal Student Aid, US Department of Education, accessed November 2014. https://studentaid.ed.gov/types/grants-scholarships/teach
15 "Iraq and Afghanistan Service Grants," Federal Student Aid, US Department of Education, accessed November 2014. https://studentaid.ed.gov/types/grants-scholarships/iraq-afghanistan-service

While grants are intended to be nonrepayable, they are not direct gift awards and may become repayable under certain conditions, such as if the recipient withdraws from a program of study.

In addition to grants, FAFSA will also be used to establish whether students can obtain work-study jobs. Both undergraduate and graduate students are eligible for employment in the federally sponsored programs.

Many states and schools use data from the FAFSA process in determining awards for their own programs, so it is a good idea to check directly with individual institutions to confirm their deadlines for application. Students need to contact their school's financial aid office to determine if they are eligible for the merit-based scholarships colleges and foundations offer to help students in specific departments or programs.

3.2 Canada

In Canada, the starting point for finding student financial assistance should start with the educational institution that the student will be attending. Institutions have financial aid officers who can help sort out a student's options and guide him or her through the application process.

In addition to school-specific scholarships for students with high grades, or bursaries and work-study programs for students in need, the federal and provincial governments offer assistance other than student loans. The federal government, for instance, offers Canada Student Grants at several different levels.[16] The Canada Student Grant for students from low-income families, for instance, pays students who have applied and qualify for financial assistance up to $250 per month to help cover costs, with low-income defined by family size and income. Students from families with higher incomes, though still modest means in a relative sense, are eligible for up to $100 per month under the Canada Student Grant for middle-income families category, again with specific family income cutoffs that vary by province and territory. Students with dependent children, disabled students, and part-time students are also eligible for similar federal grants of varying amounts.

---

16 "Canada Student Grants," CanLearn, accessed November 2014.
   http://www.canlearn.ca/eng/loans_grants/grants/

Provincial governments also maintain their own assistance programs, which are tailored to their populations and government priorities. In Ontario, for example, students can apply to the Ontario Student Assistance Program, which is the starting point for a whole range of bursaries, grants, and loans including the Canada Student Grant programs in the province. Ontario-specific programs include the first-generation bursary program, which pays $1,000 to $3,500 to students who are the first in their families to attend postsecondary education, and $300 per year distance grants for students who have to move from their family home to attend a postsecondary institution.

Ontario also has a tuition-waiver program under which the province will deduct up to 30 percent from a the tuition fees if the students meet certain family income including for students who have been away from school for up to four years. That is helpful for those students who decide to take a break from studies to work and earn money to better afford the costs of postsecondary education.

In British Columbia, the priorities for student assistance include special help to direct young people into trades and technical occupations in high demand. As with Ontario, the BC application process includes consideration for the federal Canada Student Grants. The province has developed a program that it calls the BC Access Grant for Labour Market Priorities. These are trades in which employers have found difficulties recruiting workers, and offer prospective students rewarding careers. The list of trades includes:

- Power Engineering

- Heavy Duty Mechanics

- Industrial Mechanics (Millwrights)

- Mining Industry Certificate

- Oil and Gas Field Operations

- Steamfitters and Pipefitters

- Sprinkler System Installers

- Welders and related Machine Operators

- Carpenters

- Industrial Electricians

- Heavy Equipment Operators

- Ironworkers

- Sheet Metal Workers

- Gas Fitters

The assistance students are eligible for include tool allowances, up to $4,000 in relocation assistance, grants of up to $2,000 to replace a portion of a student loan ($5,400 for students with dependent children of their own), and up to $6,500 in additional grants for students that have financial needs that exceed the maximum loan and other assistance amounts available to them. For most of the components students don't need to apply specifically for the amounts, they are evaluated for eligibility when they apply for student loans. The federal government offers additional assistance to individuals in the midst of trades training with apprenticeship incentive grants. Workers who have competed the first year of a Red Seal trade can be eligible for the $1,000 per year grants (maximum $2,000). After finishing the trade's full training, individuals may be eligible for $2,000 completion grants.

4. Trade Schools and Other Options

In establishing education savings for children or grandchildren, no one should lose sight of the career goals of the beneficiaries of such plans. Education savings isn't necessarily a race to university or college, and luckily many of the registered savings plans, particularly Canadian RESPs, are not directed just at university.

Even for parents of young adults uncertain about what they want to do, but are sitting on RESP accounts, there should be some comfort in knowing that they don't need to be in a hurry to spend the money — and they don't have to push their child into a university course they might simply drop out of. Technical or trades training can be a more viable option, particularly if the kids and their parents haven't built up savings to cover the ever-rising cost of an expensive university program.

Skilled-trades training comes with its own assistance programs, depending on where people live, and for the young person uncertain of where he or she wants to end up career wise, and offer the prospects of better employment and earnings than the more stereotypical service-sector jobs attributed to the young and underemployed.

In Canada, authorities estimate the construction sector and resource industries need to recruit hundreds of thousands of new tradespersons by 2020 to replace retiring workers and accommodate expected growth. That includes carpenters, electricians, plumbers, welders, machinists, and many other technical specialties.[17]

Trends in the US are similar with skilled trades reported to be among the most difficult positions for employers to fill and close to one fifth of America's tradespeople in the 55 to 64 demographic on the way to retirement.[18]

Apprenticeships are also tied directly to employment so they are "earn-while-you-learn" opportunities. The training is employer-sponsored, and involves 8 to 12 weeks of formal classroom education per year. For the rest of the time, apprentices learn on the job for wages that, in Canada, start at anywhere from $15 to $20 per hour and escalate on a schedule over four years until they are fully qualified journeyperson trades earning, on average, $20 to $25 per hour.[19]

While a skilled trade can wind up being a lucrative career in itself — a top-earning tradesperson can approach pay ranges in the six figures, depending on the trade — the job skills and experience can the basis for other opportunities. Significant numbers of tradespersons go into business themselves either as self-employed contractors or as a bigger firm capable of bidding on subcontracts for major construction projects.

17 "Media Resources," Careersintrades.ca, accessed October 2014.
http://www.careersintrades.ca/index.php?page=media-resources&hl=en_CA
18 "America's Skilled Trades Dilemma: Shortages Loom As Most-in-Demand Group of Workers Ages," Joshua Wright, *Forbes*, accessed October 2014. http://www.forbes.com/sites/emsi/2013/03/07/americas-skilled-trades-dilemma-shortages-loom-as-most-in-demand-group-of-workers-ages/
19 "Average Starting Salaries for Entry Level Skilled Trades Jobs," Lauren Stein, TalentEgg, accessed October 2014. http://talentegg.ca/incubator/2012/03/13/average-starting-salaries-entry-level-skilled-trades-jobs/

For the right young person, employment can be the stronger and more independent financial footing to take on university at a later stage of life. He or she can build up savings for postsecondary education. In Canada, a young person can do it through an RRSP account, which can be rolled into an official lifelong learning plan. Withdrawals retain tax-free status so long as the account-holder pays back the amount within a prescribed period after he or she finishes a degree. Coupled with previous RESP savings he or she still might have, a job in a trade can leave a young person with less debt and better able to handle bigger financial goals than his or her peers[20].

20"Lifelong Learning Plan (LLP)," Canada Revenue Agency (CRA), accessed October 2014. http://www.cra-arc.gc.ca/tx/ndvdls/tpcs/rrsp-reer/llp-reep/menu-eng.html

Chapter 6

Property

H ome ownership in North America is considered one of the central tenets of financial security. Why rent and pay someone else's mortgage when you can pay your own mortgage to wind up owning your own home? At worst, it is considered a sound way to build up savings as a mortgage loan is paid back. At best, expectations for property prices to rise over time hold the promise of increasing a young buyer's equity making his or her home a reliable investment over the long term.

However, nowhere is the financial tension between generations greater than in real estate. While parents have seen the greatest gains in property values over the last two decades, it is their children who are approaching the prospect of home ownership with higher debts and reduced spending power. In recent Canadian surveys, as many as one-third of first-time buyers reported that they needed or expected help from parents in making a purchase, and in some expensive cities, it is almost assumed that the Bank of Mom and Dad will be chipping in to the cost. In the United States, recent surveys have shown that more than a quarter of 20-something buyers relied on parents for help with a down payment.

The question is to establish whether it makes sense for parents to help their kids buy a home. For young adults just setting out on a new career, it might make more sense to rent (assuming they'll also be able to save some money) and kick-start an investment plan that would lead to home ownership later than to buy real estate before they're really ready. The magnitude of the commitment deserves taking some time to carefully consider the options.

Real estate, in investment terms, is an illiquid asset: It can't easily be converted to cash, which could hinder the ability of a 20-something owner in looking for better jobs or in accepting out-of-town promotions if he or she can't easily pick up and move. There is the risk of losing any advantage parents have given them in buying a home if they wind up having to sell just a few years later before equity gains in the property add up enough to pay back the up-front closing costs (e.g., legal fees for conveyance, inspections, mortgage insurance premiums) that go along with buying real estate. If they sell just a short time later, they can't forget that the process will involve a hefty commission to the realtor.

The rent-versus-own calculators that most financial institutions provide among their online investment tools can be useful for the 20-somethings in figuring out the answer to this question. These tools range from simple to complex. For instance, the rent-or-buy calculator offered by Canada's Office of Consumer Affairs (OCA) asks users to input a few simple bits of data: The amount saved, current rent, and the interest rate he or she would expect to pay on a mortgage. It calculates an estimate of how much a person would be able to spend on a home.[1]

The Canada Mortgage and Housing Corporation offers a more comprehensive calculator for young would-be buyers to test their financial readiness to purchasing a home. It includes worksheets that get users to lay out household expenses; add up all their debts, which is put into calculations against the accepted ratios for the amount of income they should be spending on housing (it shouldn't be more than 32 percent of pretax earnings); and the total amount of their income, which shouldn't be consumed by debt (no more than 40 per cent).[2]

In the US, the Federal National Mortgage Association, more commonly known as "Fannie Mae," also offers online resources.[3]

---

1 "Rent or Buy a Home Calculator," Office of Consumer Affairs (OCA), Industry Canada, accessed October 2014. https://www.ic.gc.ca/app/scr/oca-bc/ssc/house.html?lang=eng
2 "Homebuying Tools — Calculators," Canada Mortgage and Housing Corporation, accessed October 2014. https://www.cmhc-schl.gc.ca/en/co/buho/index.cfm
3 "Buy Overview," KnowYourOptions, Fannie Mae (Federal National Mortgage Association), accessed October 2014. http://knowyouroptions.com/buy/overview

These are estimates, but the calculations can offer a sobering suggestion about what young adults *can* afford to buy versus what they *want* to buy, and can help start a discussion about how they can get from one to the other.

It also offers a reminder that potential buyers need to be mindful of those other costs of a home purchase people don't think about when they are looking at the listing prices of homes. Using one theoretical example, putting in a suggestion of $16,000 will produce an estimate that a person could afford a $170,000 home, with just a little more than a $10,000 down payment and that about $5,100 of that hard-won savings fund will have to go toward closing costs to buy a home. The calculation offers a reminder that a buyer will face about $420 per month in ongoing costs of ownership such as property taxes and utilities. Those figures will change depending on prevailing interest rates, and obviously the amount that a curious potential buyer has to plug in, but it is helpful to ground the person's expectations.

Other calculators, such as the one offered by Get Smarter About Money[4] (produced by the Investor Education Fund founded by the Ontario Securities Commission) or the online calculator on the US National Association of Realtors' website,[5] ask for more information about interests and taxes. It will calculate whether the anticipated monthly payments to own would exceed the rent prospective buyers are paying as well as run a comparison of what equity they would earn in their expected home versus investing the amount saved for a down payment (as well as socking away the difference between their current, lower rent and the monthly cost of ownership, assuming that is attainable). In the end, prospective buyers (or committed renters) won't necessarily get the comforting, definitive yes or no answer they were looking for. It will be more like, "Not now, but at some point in the future it makes sense to buy." For the right person, who knows he or she is ready to settle down in one spot indefinitely — and has put a solid financial plan in place — home ownership is a good way to build equity.

---

4 "Buy or Rent Calculator," GetSmarterAboutMoney.ca, accessed October 2014. http://www.getsmarteraboutmoney.ca/tools-and-calculators/buy-or-rent-calculator/buy-or-rent-calculator.aspx#.VEX8ZIfQf65
5 "Rent or Buy?" US National Association of Realtors, accessed October 2014. US National Association of Realtors

Over the last few decades (except for the period of the US housing crash), buying real estate has looked like a no-brainer as an investment with steadily rising gains. There is no guarantee that today's young adults will have that same experience over the coming decades, but done right, home ownership has been a proven way of building forced savings that will serve them well. For those who can't or don't buy, the process of reaching the decision isn't about admitting defeat that they can't afford to buy; it is about making renting work for them. As long as they use the information as a means to bolster savings and investment plans, they shouldn't wind up further behind.

1. Down Payment

If the kids are established in a career and they expect to be in one place for the foreseeable future, but are still finding it tough to scrape together the elements of a home purchase and mortgage on top of student debts, a parental boost might just be the thing they need. It might simply be cosigning a loan, or as much as making a big cash gift for the down payment. Regardless of which, both parents and children need to step back and carefully consider the steps being taken.

As mentioned in Chapter 3, cosigning is not a mere formality for the paperwork. In doing so, parents are agreeing to take over payments on the loan if their children are unable to, and it can instantly change their financial position — and inadvertently so, if they do so without understanding the consequences. The lender considers the cosigners responsible as if it were their own loan, which can affect the parents credit limits and ultimately their credit score. When it comes to cosigning, depending on the parents' financial situation, it might not be a practical, or even possible, step for them to take. Kids need to understand that and not be upset if their parents are unable to help.

When it comes to the down payment, any help that parents offer can make a big difference. The more money the kids can put down, not only does it lower their monthly mortgage payments, it means that they pay less in interest over the long term leaving them with a bigger final pay off and more financial flexibility to concentrate on other financial goals.

1.1 American down payment considerations

Using the Federal Housing Administration programs for first-time buyers, a young person might be able to purchase a home with as little as 3.5 percent of the purchase price as a down payment. On a purchase of $206,000 (median across the first eight months of 2014), that would be just $7,200, but increasing it by any amount makes a considerable difference.

Using a thumbnail example of a 30-year fixed-rate mortgage at 4.1 percent means a monthly mortgage payment of $956. However, over the first 15 years, estimated interest payments will add up to $102,722. At 30 years, estimated interest payments would total $196,494. Raise that down payment to 20 percent ($41,000) and the monthly mortgage payment is brought down to $797 and interest payments add up to, $85,602 at 15 years and $122,078 at 30 years, almost 38 percent less than if the buyer just makes the minimum down payment.

1.2 Canadian down payment considerations

In many Canadian markets, an initial purchase of $320,000 would not be unheard of. In recent years, mortgage rates as low as 2.9 percent have been available. Assuming those variables on a mortgage with a five-year fixed rate and 25-year amortization, buyers paying the minimum five percent down payment of $16,000 would wind up with a monthly payment of $1,437 and pay more than $42,000 in interest before having to refinance the loan, and still be left with a balance of almost $260,000. Increasing the down payment to 10 percent ($32,000) would reduce the monthly payment to $1,361, the interest over the first five years to $39,810 and reduce the balance to be refinanced to $246,120.

Increasing the down payment to 20 percent ($64,000) is an incredible stretch, but it brings the monthly payment down to $1,210, interest over the first five years is reduced by more than $6,600 to $35,384 and leaves a balance of $218,772 to be refinanced. What's more, hitting the 20 percent threshold means the loan would no longer be considered a high-ratio mortgage requiring the borrower to also obtain mortgage insurance, which offers a buyer savings on his or her closing costs for a purchase.

2. How to Make a Contribution to the Mortgage

How a parent makes a contribution, and how the bank or mortgage lender views it, can be the tricky part. A straight-up gift of cash is the easiest. Banks will probably want to see a letter of gift stating that is what the money is, and not a loan. Even if parents do not expect repayment in the short term, a parental loan would be considered a second mortgage and banks frown on any undeclared interests in a property. It won't necessarily result in the mortgage being refused, but the lender needs to be assured about the sources of funds and any loan arrangements should be disclosed and approved first.[6]

In the American context, parents will want to consider making a gift to their child's down payment before he or she looks for a home. Banks will want to be reassured that the contribution is indeed a gift and not a loan, and it is helpful for the banks to see that the money is in the child's own account for a period of time.[7] A loan could make the child's mortgage approval more difficult, depending on what other debts he or she has.

For loans in Canada, so long as parents don't expect interest on repayment, the measure won't trigger any taxes because the money was from their after-tax funds in the first place.[8]

For American parents who intend to lend their children money in the purchase of a home, they may want to make sure the terms of the arrangement are clearly described in a contract so that the Internal Revenue Service (IRS) doesn't interpret the assistance as a gift, although that, again, will likely just wind up in more paperwork for the parents at tax time. If parents expect the kids to pay back loans with interest, that would be considered income that tax authorities expect would be declared on the parents' annual return.

If the adult child is married or in a common-law relationship, a fairly common concern is what would happen to the parents' money in the case of a divorce or the relationship ending. They

6 Interview: Real Estate Lawyer Richard Bell, Bell Alliance Lawyers & Notaries Public, Vancouver, BC, August 27, 2014.
7 "Should You Help Your Child Buy a Home? Parents Want to Do What They Can. But Sometimes They Shouldn't," Ruth Mantell, *The Wall Street Journal*, accessed October 2014. http://online.wsj.com/articles/should-you-help-your-child-buy-a-home-1402684361?cb=logged0.9967106201659927&cb=logged0.30389619138689916
8 Interview: Real Estate Lawyer Richard Bell, Bell Alliance Lawyers & Notaries Public, Vancouver, BC, August 27, 2014.

may be willing to help the couple get a leg up by buying a home, but don't want to see their gift wind up being thrown into the pool of assets split apart in the divorce or separation division of assets. One way of doing so, which requires some legal advice and the cooperation of the mortgage lender, is to register a mortgage against the property — even if it is an outright gift — to secure the funds in the event of a break up.[9]

3. Co-ownership

Co-ownership between parents and children is another route to help the younger generation own property, especially in North America's high-priced markets, and cases where mom and dad might want to keep grandchildren close.[10]

To the kids, it might feel like they are not escaping the co-living arrangement, but it allows mom and dad to share in the equity gains from rising property values.[11] As the kids' need for more room to house a growing family increases, as the parents' need for space decreases, the kids can arrange to slowly assume full ownership over time.

Parents and children don't have to live together in a co-ownership arrangement. Buying together as an investment might simply be a way to secure a mortgage for the kids. In that case, parents should not forget that this triggers a capital gains tax when the home is eventually sold. However, if parents are going into the purchase simply to help the kids qualify for the mortgage and intend their contribution to be a gift, they can structure ownership so that their interest is nominal, and work with a lawyer to place that interest in a trust for the benefit of the kids.

Parents might also have ways of leveraging the existing family home to give their children a place of their own that is close, but isn't the basement, or the childhood room that can barely contain their adult selves. Secondary suites go by many names (e.g., coach houses, granny flats, garden suites, or guesthouses), but small dwellings on the same property as a house are becoming increasingly accepted as a form of housing to help alleviate

---

9 Interview: Real Estate Lawyer Richard Bell, Bell Alliance Lawyers & Notaries Public, Vancouver, BC, August 27, 2014.
10 "First-time Buyers Bank on Mom and Dad for Help," Derrick Penner, *The Vancouver Sun*, page A1, Wednesday, March 19, 2014.
11 Interview: Real Estate Lawyer Richard Bell, Bell Alliance Lawyers & Notaries Public, Vancouver, BC, August 27, 2014.

the affordability issues being experienced in many North American cities.

In Vancouver, they are referred to as laneway houses and have been ever widely adopted as a means for house-wealthy parents to give their kids a leg up in the country's most expensive property market. The cost to build a secondary dwelling can approach $300,000, and ownership of the additional unit cannot be subdivided from the initial home. Title for a laneway home remains with the principal home owner, but financial institutions are becoming more innovative in methods of financing a secondary unit that acknowledge the family dynamic involved in building them.[12]

For a family that is close, it might be the preferred option of co-ownership, giving both parents and kids the comfort of financial security while also giving each side their own, distinctive and contained space; in other words, together, but separate. Once the financial arrangements are set and both sides have agreed about who is paying what to carry the expense of building a laneway home, it will give the kids more budget breathing room to build up their finances for full home ownership. Parents may have the option of trading places with their kids once they are ready to downsize and the kids are in the position of starting their own family (and have established more financial wherewithal to handle full home ownership). It can be beneficial to both parties, such as having grandparents close by to look after grandchildren, or kids nearby to help aging and ailing parents.

However, if parents are looking for a little more distance when they decide to reduce house size, the laneway house can still become an important factor in whether the kids are able to take over ownership of the whole property. A coach house, or laneway home, will add considerable value to a property, but the opportunity to rent it provides significant income that can factor into the calculation of whether the kids can afford to assume full ownership of the property. It won't necessarily be on a dollar-for-dollar basis, but many financial institutions will allow a high percentage of the rent a home owner is able to charge for a secondary unit as income to service a mortgage. If a secondary

---

12 " Laneway Eases Path to Ownership; Growing Trend Sees Smaller Homes Popping up Next to Larger Ones, on the Same Lot," Tracy Sherlock, *The Vancouver Sun*, page C4, Friday, May 4, 2012.

residence can be rented for $1,800 per month, for example, and the prospective buyer's bank allows them to count 90 percent of that amount as income for a mortgage application, it has the potential of dramatically beefing up the potential of the buyer's mortgage application.[13]

There are pitfalls. Owners can't look on the process casually as simply a little bit of help for their own mortgage. Renting the property is a business and needs to be treated as such. This means building financial cushions related specifically to the secondary dwelling, such as to covering gaps in income for periods when the unit isn't rented. There are additional insurance costs and emergency repair considerations such as when a washer overflows and floods the tenant's space. Owners also have to be ready for potential landlord-tenant disputes. Not all tenancies go smoothly, so landlords have to know the terms of whatever landlord-tenant laws govern their state or province, and how to use dispute-resolution tribunals under that legislation, in order to deal with those problems.

As with any transaction with the Bank of Mom and Dad, beyond any documentation that goes along with the mortgage, it is a good idea to enter into co-ownership with a solid agreement in writing about who will be responsible for what payments, and what happens in the event of unforeseen circumstances, or if living arrangements no longer work for one party or the other. It is better to have those details spelled out rather than disputing memories of who agreed to do what in verbal agreements when something goes wrong. When it comes to establishing a secondary dwelling, building such a unit is a substantial investment that can involve increasing the mortgage debt that will likely wind up being in the parents' name initially, so it isn't an arrangement that should be entered into lightly and not without an agreement in writing.

Chances are, the parents who are capable of contemplating an arrangement to help their kid purchase a home have been on the receiving end of an inheritance themselves. Considering the amount that property values have risen in some of North America's pricier markets, such as Vancouver, San Francisco, Toronto,

---

13 "How to be a landlord: A Helpful Guide for Homeowners Who Rely on Income from Suites As Mortgage Helpers," Derrick Penner, *The Vancouver Sun*, page D1, Saturday, October 5, 2013.

and New York, the death of their own parents, and sale of a family home may leave people with more freedom to be generous.

In the rare case parents might be able to buy a home for their child outright. Such generosity does come with a catch. If the parents do the buying and transfer ownership to their child, they need to be aware of the potential to trigger a tax on capital gains. In Canada, for tax purposes, Canada Revenue Agency will consider the transfer of property to have occurred at a fair market value, and any increase in that value between the purchase and handing over ownership to a child will be taxable regardless of whether the parents expect any repayment.

Chapter 7

Investments

There is conflicting data about how well the younger generations are doing when it comes to investments and savings. Some surveys by major banks indicate that millennials have positive and thrifty attitudes when it comes to saving money. They don't take it for granted that pension plans will be there for them in retirement and save accordingly. Broader demographic surveys, however, show that few are saving for retirement and that the rate that they are saving is behind what their parents were able to set aside at the same age. They know they need to save, but with less certain job prospects and higher levels of student debt, doing so is more of a struggle.

Kick-starting, or topping up, investment plans for their 20-something kids might be the best option for parents to give them the biggest long-term boost from a relatively modest upfront contribution (at least more so than the contributions required to get them into a home of their own). If they haven't started, it is a good opportunity to get their young adults into a savings plan with the potential to make those other life goals that they aren't ready for easier to handle. The question is to figure out what the best option is to do so.

Since parents will be gifting their own after-tax income to their children, it makes sense to look at starting with the tax-free savings options available in both the United States and Canada before looking at tax-deferred retirement savings plans. Such accounts don't have as generous contribution limits as retirement plans, but if parents have already paid their taxes before making a contribution, why put it into an account where the money will be subject to taxes again?

1. American Investments

In the United States, using parental help to top up registered retirement savings is complicated. For the Roth individual retirement account (IRA), investors contribute after-tax dollars and returns on the funds that are not taxed. Investors can withdraw money without penalty, at any time, but only from the amount of contributions they have made to the account, not the returns that the account has earned. They are structured as a retirement-savings tool and the real payoff is at the end when an investor is in retirement and withdrawals, referred to as "distributions," provide nontaxable income,[1]

Parents can gift money to contribute to a Roth IRA, however, the adult child has to set up his or her own account and have enough compensation from employment to establish his or her contribution limit, even if he or she is using the parents' money to contribute.[2]

There is an income-cutoff point for who is ineligible to set up a Roth IRA, but considering that as of 2014 it was $129,000 for single individuals and $191,000 for couples, that is likely not a factor that comes into play for millennials who need a little cash as a catalyst for a savings plan. American Roth IRAs also come with an annual contribution limit, which is the lesser of the earned income for 2014 or $5,500, for anyone younger than the age of 50.

The 401K accounts investments are among the most common private-sector workplace retirement savings plans. Contributions are deducted from the investor's paycheck before taxes are deducted (leaving income tax on contributed amounts to be collected on retirement). Employers often match contributions, but total deposits are capped at $17,500 per year as of 2014.[3]

---

1 " What Is a Roth IRA?" Matthew Malone, RothIRA.com, accessed October 2014. http://www.rothira.com/what-is-a-Roth-IRA
2 " Can a Parent Help an Adult Child with a Roth IRA?" Mark Kennan, Demand Media, Zacks, accessed October 2014. http://finance.zacks.com/can-parent-adult-child-roth-ira-5552.html
3 "Getting Started," 401K.com, accessed October 2014. https://nb.fidelity.com/public/nb/401k/home/get-started

The so-called traditional IRA is the personal savings equivalent, which Americans can set up and pay into along with a 401K or Roth IRA.[4] The so-called traditional IRA is another investment vehicle that is similar to the Roth in that the investor must have compensation from employment to qualify to open an IRA account, and has the same $5,500 annual contribution limit. It is unlike the Roth, however, in that contributions are tax deductible, like a 401K, but future retirement income will be taxed. Millennials looking to park a parental gift of cash need to be aware that if they intend to invest in both a Roth and traditional IRA, they will wind up splitting their annual contribution limit.

People can invest in a wide range of accounts or funds from government bonds to mutual funds (including trading in corporate stocks) so young people do need to shop for the best fees and advice to suit their needs.

For those considering more complicated investments, it is worthwhile to consult investment guides and/or seek the advice of a financial advisor in researching the best options. It is important to remember that aside from independent advisors, such as Certified Financial Planners or Registered Financial Planners, who work on a contingent-fee basis, the advisors with investment firms are also salespeople, so it is also a good idea to get a clear statement from them about their fees and how they earn their compensation from the investors' money.

2. Canadian Investments

In Canada, the tax-free option is the Tax-Free Savings Account (TFSA). The TFSA amounts to a sort of preretirement counterpart to Registered Retirement Savings Plan (RRSP) savings as a way to start accumulating a nest egg without any tax consequences. As the name implies, once deposited, the income from funds in the account — whether it is interest on savings or returns from investments — are not taxed, regardless of when an investor withdraws or uses the money. Investors can put TFSA money into a plain bank account, into investments such as Guaranteed Investment Certificates (GICs), mutual funds, or investments. They can even gamble and use a TFSA to invest in high-risk

---

4 "Who Can open a Traditional IRA?" IRS, accessed October 2014.
http://www.irs.gov/publications/p590/ch01.html#en_US_2013_publink1000254868

stocks or the stock market — matching exchange-traded funds, and even windfall returns on those investments won't be taxed.

2.1 Tax-Free Savings Account (TFSA)

As of 2013, the annual contribution limit on Tax-Free Savings Accounts (TFSAs) was $5,500. Prior to 2013 and back to 2009, the year the accounts were first authorized, the limit was $5,000, which is important knowledge because unused amounts accumulate and carry forward. That means if a young person started a TFSA in 2013, and managed to save the full $5,500, a parent could help out by paying into contributions from previous years to top up the child's TFSA total. The funds in a TFSA can also be withdrawn at any time and then redeposited, so an account is an excellent savings tool for medium-term financial goals such as saving for a wedding or major purchase such as a vehicle or new home.

Unlike retirement-savings accounts, there is no annual deadline to make TFSA contributions. Money can be deposited into a TFSA at any time; investors just need to remain mindful that they are remaining within the annual contribution limits. The rules for over-contribution are strict and can be easily triggered if investors are not careful. Say an investor has already made the maximum contribution to his or her TFSA in a given year, and then withdraws money to make a major purchase. Any amount he or she is able to redeposit within the same year will be considered an overpayment and be subject to a penalty from the Canada Revenue Agency (CRA) equivalent to 1 percent per month on the amount deposited. Investors have to wait until the following year to re-top-up their TFSA savings.

Similarly, withdrawing funds from one type of TFSA-registered account (e.g., plain savings account) and depositing it into another TFSA-registered account (e.g., stock-trading account) will be double counted as a contribution and trigger a penalty. Investors need to request direct transfers from financial institutions to move TFSA money between registered accounts.

2.2 Registered Retirement Savings Plan (RRSP)

Next in line for consideration is the Registered Retirement Savings Plan (RRSP). Parents are likely very familiar with them, their kids less so if they are just starting out, especially if they are in part-time or contract work where benefits don't include pension plans or other registered pension accounts. In that case, the younger they start, the better off they will be in terms of both establishing the habit of saving for the future and in allowing a longer period of time for the interest or returns earned on their savings to compound.

Unlike TFSAs, RRSP contributions are considered to be pre-tax income because the investors are socking away money for retirement, and as long as they don't exceed their annual contribution limit, the amount they put into an RRSP is tax deductible. That is on the understanding that investors will pay income tax on the money when they convert the fund into income when they retire. Canadians can contribute to RRSPs up to age 69, but have to turn whatever they've managed to accumulate into a Registered Retirement Income Fund (RRIF) by age 71.[5]

Also unlike TFSAs, the limit on RRSP contributions is not a fixed amount; the limit varies with the individual investor's income and is calculated and tracked by the Canada Revenue Agency (CRA) based on annual tax filings. If an individual doesn't make a contribution in a given year, or doesn't contribute to his or her limit, the unused amount carries forward. A person's annual tax-assessment form will include a notation of his or her annual limit and how much total room has accumulated. For a lot of young people who are struggling with other debts such as student loans, it might be difficult for them to also contribute to RRSPs up to the contribution limits from their own income, but they can use cash gifts from parents to top up the amount they are setting aside. All the funds, including untaxed gifts, will be subject to income tax much later, but presumably when they are in a lower tax bracket than they were in their prime earning years. In the meantime, the investors earn deductions they can claim back from income tax paid.

RRSPs also introduce young workers to the larger world of investing. They can enroll in registered retirement savings plans through their bank or credit union, or through one of dozens of other investment dealers. While they are putting away money for the future, it is not exactly like putting money into a plain savings

---

5 "RRSPs and other Registered Plans for Retirement," Canada Revenue Agency, accessed October 2014. http://www.cra-arc.gc.ca/E/pub/tg/t4040/t4040-e.html#P1168_40407

account that earns interest. Investing means paying fees to the investment firm and the salesperson or advisor they are working with for the management of their investment money. Those fees can be a little or a lot depending on whether they are putting their money into relatively simple Guaranteed Investment Certificates (GICs), such as Canada Savings Bonds, or into more aggressive investments such as mutual funds or even stocks.

Mutual fund fees can seriously eat into the investors' eventual investment returns because they are typically calculated annually based on the amount of money in the investor's account, not on the income earned from the investment. It is a good idea to start by getting a clear understanding of what fees are charged by the mutual funds investors are looking at before putting in their money.

For young people looking into more complicated investments, it is worthwhile to consult other dedicated investment guides or seek the advice of a financial advisor in researching their best options. It is important to remember that aside from independent advisors, such as Certified Financial Planners or Registered Financial Planners, who work on a contingent-fee basis, the advisors with investment firms are also salespeople, so it is also a good idea to get a clear statement from them about their fees and how they earn their compensation from the investors' money.

Chapter 8

Retirement and Aging

The last thing parents need to consider in their family's equation, but certainly not the least important, is that their retirement income has to account for costs that come along with aging. Retirement isn't just about maintaining their lifestyle into their golden years. Boomers have to be prepared for the eventuality of having to pay for more expensive services to keep up their health after they retire.

As much as the news is filled with stories about the difficulties that the young are having finding a footing, stories about the rising cost of health care for the elderly and how baby boomers aren't prepared for it are common as well. Having to deal with their own aging parents and the late-middle-age set can leave them feeling squeezed on three sides.

While earlier in the book, the prospect of baby boomers inheriting a wealth over the coming decades was discussed as a possible mitigating factor in whether parents can serve as the Bank of Mom and Dad at all, the realities of retirement might make that less advisable. Parents have seen property prices increase over the last two decades, but a prolonged period of low interest rates on investments means returns on their retirement savings have not escalated as much. Recent research in Canada hints at increasing anxiety about the end of work with 60 percent of respondents in a 2014 survey by the economic think tank the Conference Board of Canada reporting that they are worried they have not saved enough for retirement.[1]

1 "A Survey of Non-retirees and Retirees in Canada: Retirement Perspectives and Plans," Judith MacBride-King, The Conference Board of Canada, accessed November 2014. http://www.conferenceboard.ca/e-library/abstract.aspx?did=6544

In the Conference Board Survey, in the age group closest to retirement (i.e., the 55 to 64 demographic), more respondents reported that they expect to retire later, slightly past the age of 65, than younger cohorts in the research who were more optimistic about being able to call it quits by the age of 60. Within those results, 40 percent of the older demographic said they expected to return to work at least part time after their official retirement date.

One source of the anxiety of soon-to-be retirees is the expectation that they will outlive their savings. The Conference Board Survey author, Judith MacBride-King, noted that as of her writing, on average, a 55-year-old could be expected to live another 29 years to the age of 84. Regardless of whether or not boomers actually retire at or close to 65, huge numbers of boomers will hit their senior years within 20 years, and face the prospect of age-related health issues, which will come along without respect to whether or not individuals are financially prepared.

Many boomers have likely witnessed the toll long-term care has had on their own parents' finances and have seen firsthand what they need to be preparing for. Baby boomers might start their post-work lives as healthy and active as they were in the latter years of their careers, but they can expect to live longer than their parents. That will increase their risks of having to deal with diseases and health problems that go along with longer life — increased incidents of heart disease, cancer, and cognitive impairments such as dementia.

In America, the insurance holding firm Genworth reported in a 2014 report that up to 70 percent of Americans older than the age of 65 will require some form of long-term care to help them cope with failing health. The type of care can range from home-maker service and adult day programs for those still relatively independent up to assisted-living housing or outright nursing-home care for those who need constant medical care. The costs of such care aren't simply financial either, which many boomers have probably become acquainted with in looking after their own parents. The 2014 Genworth report noted that for seniors already in care, one third of their caregivers, which would include their children to a large extent, spent more than 30 hours per week looking after a loved one. A bigger number, 65 percent said they had to skip work on occasion, reduce work hours, or forego advancement as a result of needing to provide care. It is a sobering statistic for parents and their kids to consider while thinking about their more immediate futures and whether their family has the financial flexibility to offer the younger generation assistance.

Then there is the cost in dollars. Genworth calculated median rates across the US in 2014 of $43,472 per year for homemaker services up to a median of $77,380 to $87,600 annually for semiprivate or private nursing-home care.[2] Older Americans approaching retirement can expect inflation of between 1 to 3 percent per year to increase those costs by the time they are in the position of needing them with limited coverage from public programs such as Medicare to help defray expenses. That means maintaining enough income through retirement to keep up with required additional insurance or copayments for services.

---

2 "Genworth 2014 Cost of Care Survey," Genworth, accessed November 2014. https://www.genworth.com/dam/Americas/US/PDFs/Consumer/corporate/130568_032514_CostofCare_FINAL_nonsecure.pdf

Conclusion

In the final analysis, discussing whether or not a young person can make a withdrawal from the Bank of Mom and Dad should ultimately be about helping the adult child find a bridge to a more independent future. It should not result in something that further entrenches dependence on the parents' finances. Like any bank, there are limits to the resources that can be brought to bear for the purpose. Like any lender, there needs to be an application process that weighs the risk of advancing funds versus the payoff. It might be somewhat different if the parents are holding on to money that they've inherited themselves and intend to pass it on to their own adult children. Under those circumstances, they might not worry so much about exactly what use their progeny put the funds, unless there was an agreement specified in a will that it be for a specific reason that the grandkids will be expected to honor.

However, when parents are agreeing to make loans or gifts out of their own hard-earned savings, they deserve due consideration of that reality. Just because adult children are dealing with the Bank of Mom and Dad, and not a chartered bank, doesn't mean that the arrangements can be taken with a cavalier attitude. A chartered bank has considerable powers to reclaim money that isn't being paid back that have real consequences to borrowers that are in default. The Bank of Mom and Dad won't have the same recourse, but they are taking a more tangible risk than banks in not being repaid. A large bank has the ability to write off bad loans as part of its business. Parents will live more closely with the reality of having to work longer than they antici-pated or forego one of their own goals to make up the difference if their child winds up not being able to pay them back.

Being open and transparent is key in such discussions and hopefully this book has offered some tools that kids and par-ents can use to arrive at practical financial plans for achieving goals. Whether it is taking a next step in postsecondary educa-tion, helping a son or daughter take a first step on the property ladder, or putting seed money into a college-savings fund for the grandchildren, the kids have to be part of the solution. The kids might have enjoyed a worry-free upbringing with all of their needs looked after, but mom and dad won't be around forever to keep that expectation going. The adult children should real-ize that the parents are likely not too far removed in space and time from an era when there were no public pensions and where the social safety net was the expectation that the kids would be the ones looking after parents in their old age. Given the aging of North America's population, millennials might not be that far away from that reality again.

There are more options for parents to offer financial assis-tance to their adult children than there will be financial resourc-es to tap into doing so. All of them may be a big help to the kids, but in the end, both sides have to be prepared for the eventuality that none of them will be possible. Starting the discussion about being the Bank of Mom and Dad isn't about developing expecta-tions; it is an exercise in determining a reasonable reality.

It is true that in the post-recession environment, the cur-rent generation of young adults is having a hard time getting its footing. However, their parents lived through the recession too, which dealt them setbacks of their own in terms of damaged investments or unexpected changes in their employment. Kids might look at their parents and see them living a comfortable lifestyle, but parents might be more focused on the few remain-ing work years they have before retirement and whether they themselves have saved enough.